Early Praise for *C*

In *Can You Sleep Like This? In the Rest of God*, Evonne Thompson has found the perfect balance of wit and wisdom. Her humorous accounts of her own attempts at achieving a stress-free and restful life echo the sometimes embarrassing and often hopeful experiences we all create when we are just too tired and worn out to move another inch! Yet, mixed with these amusing anecdotes are fresh ponderances on the wisdom of the Bible and the desire God has for each of us to realize the peace and comfort of God's plan for our lives. In this tapestry of scholarly work and worldwide experience, Evonne Thompson provides a respite for our weariness with the theological, mental, and spiritual help we all need to "sleep like this, in the rest of God."

Reverend Dr. Rosa M. Sailes
Founder of The EZRA Project
Chicago, Illinois

Can You Sleep Like This? by Dr. Evonne Thompson is an excellent book for everyone who wants to sleep like a baby! Sleep is one of the precious blessings from God. We can live without food for weeks, but we cannot sustain our body for long without sleep or rest. This book will capture your heart and mind through a solid biblical foundation and the Holy Spirit as Evonne shares the power of prayer in the midst of the challenges of life. I highly recommend this book, for it will teach you to rest in God!

Dr. SueLee Jin
Pastor-Salem Campus, Anderson Hills
Cincinnati, Ohio

If the year 2020 has taught us anything, it has taught us that change is inevitable. Dealing with the "tri-demic" changes of disease, social unrest, and financial uncertainty have led us to have many sleepless moments. In spite of all of this, we have hope for rest. In her provocative book *Can You Sleep Like This? In the Rest of God*, Evonne Thompson gives us humorous yet insightful and spiritual prescriptions of how to find rest in God. If you're looking for ways to overcome seasons of spiritual insomnia, this book is a must-read!

Reverend J. Elvin Sadler, D.Min.
Assistant Dean for Doctoral Studies,
United Theological Seminary, Dayton, Ohio
General Secretary–Auditor, The A.M.E. Zion Church
Charlotte, North Carolina

Unprecedented times required unprecedented resources. In the face of a global pandemic, economic uncertainty, churches closing by the thousands, and hopelessness at an all-time high, there could not be a more perfect time for this book. Evonne Thompson delivers a masterpiece! There is a rest for the people of God. This book is a home run. Life is different for those who experience the rest of God.

C. Terrell Wheat
Associate Pastor, Director of Prayer, New Life Covenant Southeast
Chicago, Illinois

Can You Sleep Like This? In the Rest of God, Dr. Evonne Thompson's book, already provokes peace in the heart of the reader. Rest was a fundamental part of the creative agenda. God rested after the work of creation and calls humanity into a life of rest. If there were ever a time in the history of mankind when hearts are calling for rest, that time is now, and that makes the timing of this book priceless. The author is very well educated in issues of divinity and also in the corporate world. She has seen the pain and struggle of many in corporate America and coming from a scriptural perspective, shows the reader amazing possibilities of finding rest and peace in the arms of the "Prince of Peace." Everyone who wants to live a life of trust and rest, in spite of our sometimes chaotic world, ought to grab a copy and read. Highly recommended.

Reverend Dr. George Mike Portuphy
National Youth Pastor,
The Rehoboth Pentecost International Worship Center
Wayne, New Jersey

I am thrilled to recommend *Can You Sleep Like This? In the Rest of God* by my friend Dr. Evonne Thompson. Drawing from her personal experiences, she exposes in great depth the devastating impact that occurs as a result of living one's life in constant unrest, anxiety, and fear. Dr. Thompson offers valuable biblical insights to help us practically overcome time challenges, adjust poor sleeping habits, and even awaken our heart to His wooing. In this book, she lays the groundwork for developing essential spiritual disciplines as a way to reestablish the Lord's pathway for rest in our life. I believe the truths within these pages are vital and will usher in a significant spiritual transformation to those who read this book.

Darrian A. Summerville, Sr.
Founder & Senior Pastor, City Servants Church
Manassas, Virginia

Rest is an important part of a healthy life—so important, in fact, that God commands it in the Bible. In this readable book, Dr. Thompson provides useful advice, based on personal experience and biblical teaching, on how to rest well and live the life that God intends for us.

David F. Watson, PhD
Academic Dean & Vice President for Academic Affairs
Professor of New Testament, United Theological Seminary
Dayton, Ohio

Here's a rhetorical question, "Do you need more rest?" I think everyone would resoundingly answer "Yes!" In Evonne Thompson's new book, *Can You Sleep Like This? In the Rest of God*, you'll discover reasons your sleep and rest are interrupted and how you can overcome negative sleep patterns affecting your rest. You'll learn godly principles to overcome worry and live in peace, ensuring better sleep and remaining in His rest.

Dr. Bob Sawvelle
Founder & Senior Pastor, Passion Church
Tucson, Arizona
Author of Receive Your Miracle Now!, Fulfill Your Dreams, *and* Our Eyes Are on You

Dr. Evonne Thompson has written a book for a time like this. A woman of great faith, she shares her experience as a Christian in the busy and rushed marketplace and teaches how to find peace and rest by laying down our troubles before God. She teaches us that God ordains rest and that it is for us. This book is a must-read for Christians seeking tranquility, especially amid uncertainties and questions for what is to come in their lives.

Sang Sur, PhD, ThD
Chief Executive Officer, Sciturus Real Investment Group
President, Prayer Tents

Can You Sleep Like This?

In the Rest of God

DR. EVONNE THOMPSON

Printed in the United States of America
First Printing Edition, 2021
Paperback ISBN 9781736311110
Hardback ISBN 9781736311127
eBook ISBN 9781736311103

Library of Congress Cataloging-in-Publication Data

Names: Thompson, Evonne, author.
Title: Can you sleep like this? : in the rest of God / Evonne Thompson.
Description: First Printing edition. | Salt Lake City : Izzard Ink Publishing, 2021.
Identifiers: LCCN 2021009345 | ISBN 9781736311110 (paperback) |
ISBN 9781736311127 (hardback) | ISBN 9781736311103 (epub)
Subjects: LCSH: Rest—Religious aspects—Christianity. |
Sleep—Religious aspects—Christianity. |
Stress management—Religious aspects—Christianity. |
Spiritual life—Christianity. | Spirituality—Christianity.
Classification: LCC BV4597.55 .T46 2021 | DDC 248.4—dc23
LC record available at https://lccn.loc.gov/2021009345

IZZARD INK
PUBLISHING

To my parents, Bishop Winston and the late Mrs. Mary Thompson, who came from a generation characterized by staunch integrity, loyalty, hard work, and faithfulness. Aside from my relationship with God, you set an incredible foundation that encouraged and facilitated the process to excel. Thank you for your indelible love and support.

To my big sisters, Bonnie Wilson and the late Marilyn Hester, who overwhelmingly laughed with me, supported, and covered me through every over-the-top and cheeky response given to life's challenges and some of its inhabitants. Psalm 126:1–3.

Acknowledgements

Thank you, Denise Graham, for being a reliable friend over the years and providing consistent support and assistance from start to finish of this work.

Thank you to my friends, Gary Parker (@parkerspicsinsta) and Glenda Jack, who worked with me to provide photography for the book cover and other media.

Contents

Foreword

RARELY DOES ONE FIND A BOOK LIKE DR. THOMPSON'S that breaks into a neglected but important aspect of the Christian life, in this case the power of resting in the presence of God.

I was raised in a fundamentalist Christian culture that emphasized diligence and unrelenting hard labor. Taking a nap or vacation was seen as laziness and shirking "the Lord's work." I often heard, "How long wilt thou sleep, O sluggard? when wilt thou arise out of thy sleep? Yet a little sleep, a little slumber, a little folding of the hands to sleep: So shall thy poverty come as [a robber], and thy want as an armed man" (Proverbs 6:9–11). A favorite hymn was "Work for the Night Is Coming." It was emphasized that Jesus did not waste His time sleeping, but He spent His nights praying—and so should we.

Well, there's room for all that diligence, of course, but the Bible also provides balance on the issue of work vs. rest. Dr. Thompson's work lays out the appropriateness of rest in the presence of God, even during stressful times—just as Jesus did—asleep in a storm-tossed boat. This work invites us to follow the model of God him-self: "for whoever has entered God's rest has also rested from his works as God did from his. Let us therefore strive to enter that rest so that no one may fall by the same sort of disobedience." Resting in the presence of God, Dr. Thompson rightly argues, properly refuels and rejuvenates our soul, a practice that is also an act of service to the Father.

Jon Ruthven, PhD
Professor Emeritus, Regent University,
PhD director, Iris University,
Author of Should Jesus Be Allowed to Define Christianity?
(2021)

Introduction

I HAVE A CONFESSION TO MAKE. AS AN EDUCATED PERSON with an adult son, sometimes I am afraid of the dark. Sometimes I sleep with the light on. Sometimes I am nervous I will see something. A lot of times it is due to my overactive imagination that acts up at times during the day, but really shows off and works overtime in the dark.

But most often, it is because I cannot sleep, and it makes me feel better to keep a dim light on as I lie awake trying to fall asleep. Sometimes it is due to a hundred thoughts (often a thousand) whirling around in my head. Sometimes my head is so full of the day's concerns that my thoughts do not stop automatically when it is time for bed. Other times some crisis, or situation weighs on my mind.

What are you afraid of seeing in the dark? Maybe it's your mother-in-law or father-in-law? Maybe it's finding your teenager out on a night crawl, or even how you look under your pajamas?

Regardless of the reasons, the causes produce like results—the inability to fall asleep, sleep well, or sleep at all. For others, the issue may be oversleeping or the excessive desire to sleep too much. Sleep can be an escape from reality and an indirect coping mechanism to handle life. At times, contributing factors, such as one's health, an inadequate mattress, or other extenuating circumstances, can be the problem. But our mental, emotional, and spiritual state can correlate to our capacity to get a good night's sleep. If life is good, then we may rest well, but if things are not going well, then our sleep patterns may be negatively impacted.

Navigating life, whether one is a believer of God or not, involves constant pressures, concerns, trouble, trials, and even persecutions. On top of external influences such as jobs, church, finances, relationships, and even societal, community, and racial tensions, there is also the spectrum of internal forces that pressure us, such as our self-construct, emotions, and mental state. As believers, we may face further complexity and pressure due to spiritual battles. Although we may experience many blessings from God, life is generally not a bed of constant happiness and bliss. Sometimes it is like a hard, lumpy, indented mattress on which one consistently struggles to get comfortable.

This book is written from a Christian perspective. It uses the metaphor of sleep to address and provide guidance on entering the rest of God. The metaphor serves as a means to bring out, discuss, and link scriptural principles. For example, you may be able to sleep extremely well regardless of the difficult situations you face. This is a great feat, considering so many people do not. However, you may instead suffer from other coping mechanisms unrelated to sleep, such as overeating, television and social media bingeing, excessive drinking, or even the use of recreational drugs. But the principles set out throughout the subsequent chapters are still applicable to you. Your coping mechanism is interchangeable with the sleep metaphor comparison.

What Keeps You Up at Night?

Although the idea to write a book about the principles of rest came several years prior to the 2020 pandemic, I never had the opportunity to buckle down and write it until I went through a very unsettling season. Interestingly, this season was not nearly as tough as other seasons of extreme difficulty I'd experienced in the years immediately prior to it. I find it ironic that the opportunity came to write during the pandemic—a time characterized by great fear, anxiety, and stress. I write this book as a source of encouragement, using light-hearted anecdotes that hopefully lift the spirit.

I was unemployed for several months during the pandemic, which was extremely unsettling, but I did not allow it to rob me of my faith, perseverance, or joy in God as I plowed through with focus and tenacity. Think about the things that you are struggling with currently. It may be the continued aftereffects from the 2020 pandemic. It may involve the death of loved ones. Are your children causing you significant ire? Is your marriage on a downward spiral, and it seems unredeemable? A terminal illness for you or someone in your family? Maybe it is a job loss, foreclosure, bankruptcy, or even housing issues. Whatever we must face, often our circumstances can overwhelm us, and we feel ill-equipped to persevere and endure. Faith, hope, and peace escape us.

If you have problems resting because of those types of issues, incorporating God's principles and wisdom consistently and persistently in your life will transform you. Proverbs 3:21–24 teaches us this: "Keep sound wisdom and discretion, So they will be life to your soul And adornment to your neck. Then you will walk in your way securely And your foot will not stumble. When you lie down, you will not be afraid; When you lie down, your sleep will be sweet."

As time progresses, I believe the intensity of life will continue to increase. Trials will increase. Natural disasters and their impact on people will get worse. Believers need to be able to stand and endure. The pandemic taught me that as believers we need to be securely grounded in our faith, with little room to be swayed by the huge array of false information, manipulative news programs, and deceptive data routinely skewed based on vested interests. According to Ecclesiastes 1:9, there is nothing new under the sun. Despite the increased testing that will come, the Bible still offers respite through utilization of its principles that continue in their relevance today.

Can You Sleep Like This? examines key tenets identified and reviewed in Scripture related to the principle of rest. As a seminary-trained educator, I applied exegetical consideration at a high level to the concept of rest across the Bible, from the Old Testament to the New Testament. Chapters 1 to 4 lay a scriptural foundation for a detailed review of the principles. You may find these chapters a bit more technical. Chapters 5 to 9 discuss spiritual and practical factors. This study is not an exhaustive theological or academic examination. Instead, it seeks to draw believers into a deeper understanding of God's desire for them to enter His rest and experience greater peace in the midst of life's hardships.

The end of every chapter includes three components: Reflect, Response, and Rest. Questions are posed in the Reflect section to help you reflect on the areas that impact your ability to rest as discussed in the chapter. Response statements reiterate either key principles or scriptures from the chapter that encourage you to think about them and respond. And finally, the Rest section includes a scripture and prayer related to the chapter designed to lead you into quiet time with God, where you can rest a few moments in His presence. When applied consistently, this exercise will produce great fruit. However, please note there are no quick wins. It is for the long haul.

By the end of this study, you will have tools you can incorporate as you steer through the difficulties of your life and to steer without feeling fearful, stressed-out, or hopeless. I invite you on a journey through this study to embrace a deeper level in God that will increase your fruitfulness, productivity, and peace in every aspect of your life

What keeps you up at night? What do you fear? What are the struggles you face that make you feel stressed and anxious? When you lie down, is your sleep sweet? Can you sleep in the rest of God?

CHAPTER ONE

Take a Break

W E NEED TO TAKE A BREAK. TAKE A LOAD OFF, chill, relax, release.

As a type-A personality who worked in Big Four public accounting firms where many of my clients were part of the Fortune 200, I didn't grasp the concept of taking a break. My week as a director consisted of fifty-five-plus hours of work (sometimes upwards of seventy). I was always available by cell or email, and taking conference calls on the weekend was the norm. I traveled for work so much that most years I achieved platinum status with airline and hotel award programs. I can recall several times literally stepping out of Sunday morning worship or weekly Bible class to take calls because the partner or client had to address an issue immediately—and for some reason could never wait until the next day.

I cannot recall one vacation in a ten-year time frame where I was completely free from taking conference calls, responding to emails, or addressing client requests or deliverables, irrespective of time zones. Whether in Europe, Asia, or other parts of the United States, I used my fingers a lot to calculate the correct time zones for making calls or attending meetings to ensure I did not mistakenly miss them. What a great relief it was to learn of the World Clock feature on iPhone.

I could never relax or get proper rest, even on vacation, unless I was fortunate to plan one for more than seven days, which was rare. I remember during one family trip overseas, every night after we finished touring and sightseeing, I still had to stay up a few hours on US time to answer emails and perform client work. On one hand, I would never complain, considering the blessing it was to be on vacation with my family. On the other hand, working daily while on vacation and only getting minimal sleep or rest was not ideal either.

Then one day I had an epiphany. I realized if I was fired or resigned, the company would still carry on. If I were no longer there, they would hire someone else to replace me. I was killing myself to move up the corporate ladder and appease a secular paradigm, but at what expense? What was the value of working sixty-plus hours a week, jumping on planes almost weekly, and flying to client locations to meet numerical quotas if it could jeopardize my health, weight, spiritual walk, family life, and emotional well-being?

Many colleagues had full-time nannies to help care for their children and were unable to spend the time they needed or wanted with them. Some colleagues compromised their integrity and character for promotions. I witnessed numerous instances of egregious competitiveness, cronyism, the old boys' network, acute greed, and even a few instances of infidelity, in order to advance careers or simply to be liked or validated by superiors.

After my revelation, I decided to take charge of my time and pursue work-life balance. No longer would I look at or respond to email after a certain time in the evening during the week. On the weekend, even if I looked at my email, since I used one cell phone for both work and personal, I stopped responding to work emails. I also started to use the handy Do Not Disturb feature on my iPhone, which silences your phone during certain times (but allows urgent calls or calls from designated people to go through). No longer would I be jarred awake from people calling from the Eastern time zone while I was on Pacific time, or vice versa.

Over the next couple years, as I tried to consistently incorporate those habits into my life, I noted a key lesson. I learned that more work hours in a day does not equate to more productivity or better quality. In fact, it leads to the opposite. Often, we sacrifice sleep or proper rest in order to maximize the available hours in a day. However, we can end up being counterproductive instead, due to being overworked, stressed, and anxious as we try to get an overload of things done in one day or one week. We take longer to do tasks due to fatigue or lack of sleep, and inevitably we make mistakes or end up with mediocre results.

Toilet Naps

Current custom adheres to a five-day work week and a two-day weekend. Considering there are many jobs that are not conducted Monday through Friday, a weekend can be inclusive of any day or two of one's day(s) off to be classified as the same. Weekends should be a chance for one to spend time with family, connect with friends, and rejuvenate from the hustle and bustle of the work week, while at the same time prepare for the next week. However, from what I know of many people, they work on the weekend in some form while still having to juggle countless activities, chores, and familial obligations, so that a two-day weekend may only deliver a few hours of rest, as opposed to at least one full day. People are overworked, tired, stressed, fearful, anxious, and overwhelmed, which is often exacerbated by a lack of sufficient rest and sleep.

I have always been aggressive and an overachiever. If a new qualification or credential is established for my current job or role, I feel compelled to achieve it. At one point in time, although I already had two master's degrees and was a certified public accountant, I decided to pursue the CFA (chartered financial analyst) qualification. At that time, the CFA took three years to complete with three exams, the last two exams being offered only once a year. So if you failed, you had to wait an entire year to retake it. Thus, a three-year process could become a part-time career for multiple years of test taking. I was on the part-time career trajectory. In hindsight, I did not need the qualification, but at the time I felt it was beneficial and essential to my career.

During that time, I held a full-time position overseeing a department and worked over forty hours a week. I was involved in my church, where I regularly taught and served. I also was a parent of a teenager. Studying for the exam required about six months of my time on top of everything else I had to do. My plan was to study every night after work and on the weekend, aside from nights I was at the church. Needless to say, I was all over the place.

To make up for my lack of rest, my life became uncomfortable and my need for sleep caused me to be in precarious and delicate situations at work. I found myself sometimes sleeping in the bathroom stall designated for users with handicaps to make up for my lack of sleep at night. I would make a pallet on the floor with my blazer and take a nap. How pitiful is that? Have you ever tried to fall asleep on a cold tiled floor in the middle of the day while at work? Let me tell you, it is not comfortable—at all. It becomes even more uncomfortable when someone knocks on the door, then annoyingly stands and waits outside the door to subliminally pressure you to hurry up. One—can I please have some privacy? And two—how do you hurry up taking a nap in the bathroom? Despite turning my life upside down, endangering my day job, and feeling like I was not properly meeting my obligations as a church member, a mother, and a friend, I did not pass the exam and that, too, was due to insufficient rest.

Sleep depravity and the lack of rest plague many people for varying reasons. For some people, both tend to be optional based on one's lifestyle, i.e., they choose not to take time out for resting or believe it is fine to operate on as little sleep as possible. Some people lack sleep due to health reasons, others due to heavy workloads that compete with demanding obligations, whether it is family, business, ministry, or other commitments. For many, the inability to sleep or take a break on a recurring basis is normal, and in some circles, it's even frowned upon.

Sometimes we may feel tired but are not necessarily sleepy. This is because rest and sleep, though closely related, are slightly different. The next chapter delves in greater detail on the concept of rest. But in regard to sleep, it is a necessary component of rest. We can rest without sleeping, but when we sleep it is a part of the resting process.

Sleep as a metaphor symbolizes rest and contributes to our understanding of its importance. Rest starts as a principle, with key tenets occurring throughout Scripture, from Genesis to Revelation. In the Old Testament, God rested; and in the New

Testament, Jesus slept. This is important to know, as I believe rest as a spiritual discipline is heavily underutilized compared to other spiritual disciplines. This is not to say that rest is more important than prayer, praise, or worship, but it certainly should be a priority in every believer's spiritual walk.

A lack of proper rest contributes to a number of risks. From a natural perspective, a lack of physical rest, sleep, or both can create a number of health and medical challenges. According to the National Sleep Foundation, "Sleep loss puts a person at risk for heart disease, heart attack, and heart failure, as well as irregular heartbeat, high blood pressure, stroke, and diabetes."[1] While we sleep, a number of restorative activities occur that contribute to our mental and physical well-being. Restorative functions such as tissue repair, muscle growth, and release of toxins take place while we sleep.[2]

Every night our body needs time to go through the restorative process. When this does not consistently occur, we put our bodies at risk for an accumulative detrimental effect over time. It is only while sleeping, versus resting, that our cells repair, and applicable internal organs obtain the reprieve needed to recuperate.

A lack of consistent rest also impacts us spiritually. We are unable to be as alert or vigilant when we do not rest well. Our discernment can become dulled, affecting our ability to hear from God clearly or to endure testing. Our spiritual walk suffers over time because we constantly feel drained or overwhelmed, with minimal feeling or demonstration of the joy of the Lord in our relationship with Him. Even from a spiritual perspective,

1 National Sleep Foundation, "What Is Insufficient Sleep?" https://www.sleep.org/insufficient-sleep/.

2 National Sleep Foundation, "How Sleep Works," https://www.sleep.org/sleep-for-mind-and-body/.

we need time to rest: to repair, restore, relieve, refresh, reset, and release.

———

Rest: Repair. Restore. Relieve. Refresh. Reset. Release.

———

Lumpy Mattresses

For some reason, no one in my family ever wants to share sleeping arrangements with me. According to them, and I feel this is wildly exaggerated, I am a horrible sleeper. They have shared claims of seeing me fast asleep while hanging halfway off the bed in the middle of the night, or sleeping at a nearly 180-degree angle in the bed. According to my twin sister, I have a tendency to flail my arms and legs sporadically and repeatedly throughout the night. I am not sure what makes them say such things, but I get the pleasure of not having to share a bed, along with the punishment of always getting the lumpy mattress, the cot, or when I was younger, the floor.

As a result, I am a self-conscious sleeper if I have to share sleeping arrangements. I am amazed by people who can fall asleep anywhere, anytime. And I'm not talking about gentle little nod-offs, but literally falling into a deep sleep, like in the middle of family gatherings with twenty-plus adults and kids laughing and talking, as well as the television blasting. Ironically, Jesus had such an ability, as described in the Gospels.

Matthew 8:23–27 is an appealing scripture. It tells the story of how Jesus fell into a deep sleep. Interestingly, it is also repeated in the Gospels of Mark and Luke, which suggests key importance and relevance. The passage tells the story of the disciples and Jesus in a boat out at sea when a horrible storm ensues. This is the part of the passage that is most known to believers.

However, what I find interesting are a couple of elements I did not notice before. Jesus is the one who initiated going into the boat. The disciples are the ones who followed Him into the boat. If Jesus was both man and divine, surely He knew prior to getting into the boat that an impending deadly storm would soon occur, right? Surely, He knew of the trouble and the danger that would occur if the disciples followed Him, did He not? The trouble would be terrifying, and difficult, but He still told them to follow Him.

Verse 24 says, "And behold, there arose a great storm on the sea, so that the boat was being covered with the waves; but Jesus Himself was asleep." He told them to follow Him, and then He got into the boat and fell asleep. This happens to all of us! We are following Him. We are seeking Him. We are calling on Him. We are doing everything we know to do, and it feels as if nothing is happening, nothing is changing, or moving for our benefit or on our behalf. It feels like God is not listening or, as in this story, is fast asleep and not seeing or not in touch with what is happening in our lives.

And considering He was man and divine, it still puzzles my mind why He needed to sleep, or how He slept. Did He ever snore or sleep with His mouth hanging open? If He were sleeping so deeply that He could not even hear the waves slapping across the boat, perchance He was snoring and that is why He could not hear the commotion overhead. Based on the high decibels of noise I have heard from some of my family members during the night, this could be a possible scenario.

My common reaction to this family scenario, depending how much I am traumatized by the culprit, is normally to yell, hit the person with a pillow, slam a door, or if it's a younger person, hit them with a very strong "love" tap or yank their sheet or pillow. Verse 25 simply says, "they came to Him, and woke Him, saying, 'Save us Lord; we are perishing!'" I think I prefer my process of waking better—a vigorous, repetitive shaking and a holler, "Get the heck up! You're the Messiah for God's sake (pun intended) why on earth are you even sleeping? You're not supposed to slumber or sleep! Get up, man, we're gonna die!"

But as a man, perhaps Jesus slept so soundly because He knew the source of peace that resided within. He held the power to rebuke the winds and the sea and instill perfect calm (verse 26). When He speaks, even the winds and water must obey. "Then He arose and rebuked the wind, and said to the sea, 'Peace, be still!' And the wind ceased and there was a great calm" (Mark 4:39, NKJV).

———

But Jesus Himself was asleep.
Matthew 8:24

———

The disciples focused on what they saw of the storm around them, that it was perilously encroaching and invading their territory. They did not consider the cargo present with them on the boat. The storm overshadowed their knowledge of the person they not only followed but who was also right there with them. While the disciples worried and panicked, they neglected to recognize that they carried the source of ultimate rest and calm with them. How could the boat possibly go down?

Both believers and nonbelievers may sleep well. And both may not sleep well. However, we can improve and experience true rest in God if we believe and abide in Him and He abides in us. This is the starting point—we must accept Him as our Lord, and then we choose to follow Him. When we follow God, it may mean that we follow Him through seasons of storms, turbulent times, or uncertain waves. It may appear that He is not listening or in touch with what we are going through. However, He is in the boat with us. He is present. He is near. And He is with us.

Reflect

* *What are your sleep patterns? Do you have trouble sleeping?*

* *What are the things that keep you up at night?*

* *How do your sleep patterns impact your work life? Spiritual life? Family life?*

Response

Respond and journal how the following key principles applies to or impacts you.

* *"But Jesus Himself was asleep" (Matthew 8:24).*

* *"Then He arose and rebuked the wind, and said to the sea, 'Peace, be still!' And the wind ceased and there was a great calm" (Mark 4:39, NKJV).*

* *Rest: Repair. Restore. Relieve. Refresh. Reset. Release.*

Rest

"Then He arose and rebuked the wind, and said to the sea, 'Peace, be still!' And the wind ceased and there was a great calm."

Mark 4:39

Lord, thank you for the opportunity to learn more of you. Help me to follow you into the storms and crashing waves that you allow to come into my life. Help me to recognize your presence and be aware of how you choose to be near me. Teach me how to stand with your authority to speak to and rebuke the storms while I rest in you.

CHAPTER TWO

All Work and No Play?

A S PART OF MY QUEST TO TAKE A BREAK AND TAKE
charge of my work schedule and my health, I knew I
needed to get more exercise. Given my travel schedule and several
unsuccessful attempts to join a gym, I decided to take up hiking
after enjoying a leisurely walk in a beautiful local park.

After a bit of research, I found a couple of local hiking groups.
After my first group hike, I recognized it was something I could
do regularly on the weekends. Time on the trails would provide
low-impact exercise; fresh air; opportunities to experience beautiful parks; space for mental breaks from work demands, laptops,
clients, and meetings; and time for spiritual, emotional, and personal respite.

A member of the hiking group suggested a backpacking trip.
I signed up to go before it sank into my overachiever brain that
I had never backpacked before, or even camped. But the adven-
turous side of me kicked in, along with my research side, and I
decided to take a camping/backpacking overnight class before my

scheduled trip so I could be well-prepared for the group hike. I was both excited and incredibly nervous on the class day.

As the class hike progressed, I pondered, *What company picks a park for a beginner's overnight that does not allow campfires in the middle of October?* The excitement wore off as night descended—at five-thirty—in the middle of a national park forest, where I could not turn on any light, under all the forest trees where little light came through.

When I asked the guide if we could shine our headlamps and continue with our group camaraderie since it was only six o'clock, I was told we should go to bed, i.e., our tents. Sheer terror set in. Twelve hours laid ahead until light would peek through the trees. I faced a conundrum of leaving my little lamp on through the night and attracting the wild animals and forest people, or turning it off so that the battery did not run out in the event I needed to use the bathroom during the night. I erred on the side of caution and chose the latter.

I prayed. I sang (quietly) every praise and worship song that came to my mind. I pleaded to the Lord vigorously for hours. I needed protection from the darkness, from all the wild animals waiting to devour me, and from the people who lived in the forest who wanted to capture me. When I realized I had to use the bathroom several hours later, I travailed harder. Because of wisdom I decided it best not to leave the tent before I could see daylight. I told my Father if He helped me to wait until dawn to use the bathroom, I would try my best to never again embroil myself in such nonsensical foolishness and instead use a treadmill like normal people.

Because He loves me, at some point past four in the morning, I finally drifted off to sleep for a couple of hours until daybreak, when it was safe to leave the tent. It also helped that I intentionally and purposely put my tent in the middle of everyone else's. In the event we were attacked by a bear or wild animals, my peers would be their initial targets while giving me a head start to put on my glasses, unzip my sleeping bag, put on my jacket and shoes, unzip my tent, and then run like the dickens.

Power to Produce

Nearly all of my anxiety and alarm were unfounded and based on a lack of exposure, awareness, and knowledge. This happens too in our walk with God and how we live. It is important to know God's Word and its applicability to our experiences, to discern His voice and His will in our circumstances. Psalm 119:105 says, "Your word is a lamp to my feet And a light to my path."

The next few chapters may come across as a bit technical as I share several biblical principles. I do not want to rely solely on personal stories but on the foundation of God's Word. Your story may be different from mine, but His Word and its principles remain the same. I hope you will also embrace this approach.

In Scripture the first mention of a concept can highlight key information or underlying principles that still apply when repeated subsequently throughout the Bible. In the book of Genesis, we see the first mention of the word *rest*. It appears not only as a simple word, but also recurrently as a key principle throughout Scripture in varied ways. This chapter explores how the first use of the word in Genesis (and its applicability) demonstrates a standard God originally intended and required for His people.

According to the Genesis account, in the beginning God created the heavens and the earth. Across that time frame, He performed a series of activities that involved creating something from nothing. The list below describes the types of activities He performed in Genesis 1 as He engaged the environment into action:

- moved over the waters

- separated light from darkness

- made the expanse and distinguished it from the waters

- gathered the waters to distinguish them from dry land

- brought forth vegetation, plants that yielded seeds

- established fruit trees that bore fruit

- spoke forth living creatures

- blessed His work

For each creative activity, He spoke or called something into being to produce something. The only exception occurred in Genesis 1:26 and 2:7. Here, He went a step further and physically formed man, as opposed to only speaking him into existence:

- Genesis 1:26—Then God said, "Let Us make man in Our image, according to Our likeness; and let them rule over the fish of the sea and over the birds of the sky and over the cattle and over all the earth, and over every creeping thing that creeps on the earth."

- Genesis 2:7—Then the Lord God formed man of dust from the ground, and breathed into his nostrils the breath of life; and man became a living being.

Creative power to speak forth structure from chaos, fruit from barrenness, and light from darkness.

Regardless of the original form, each activity depicts God's creative energy and reflects His nature and predisposition to produce. God's inherent nature is to bring forth potential, create life, and bear fruitfulness. He possesses the power to create despite conditions that are "formless and void" or where "darkness was over the surface. . . ." (Genesis 1:2). He can create and call forth structure and organization out of chaos and barrenness. He can move amid darkness and bring forth light to separate darkness from light that He creates or brings forth.

Genesis 1 describes a series of activities God performed, such as "Then God said," or "and there was." But in chapter two, it is the first time the total of these acts is actually referred to as work. The second verse says, "God completed His work" and "He rested on the seventh day from all His work." *Merriam-Webster's Dictionary* defines work as "to perform or carry through a task requiring sustained effort or continuous repeated operations," or "to exert oneself physically or mentally especially in sustained effort for a purpose or under compulsion or necessity."[3]

---

3 *Merriam-Webster*, s.v. "work (*n.*)," https://www.merriam-webster.com/dictionary/work.

Paid Time Off

The first chapter of Genesis depicts a bustle of activity, energy, and power initiated by God, but when we move to chapter 2, a shift occurs. Chapter 2 describes a halt to the work in Genesis 1—a pivot from the flurry of activity and work, to an emphasis that God stopped and rested from the work He did. The passage in Genesis 2:1–3 reads:

> Thus, the heavens and the earth were completed, and all their hosts. By the seventh day God completed His work which He had done, and He rested on the seventh day from all His work which He had done. Then God blessed the seventh day and sanctified it, because in it He rested from all His work which God had created and made.

If you consider saying "Let there be" over and over as a requirement for sustained effort, then potentially it would merit rest. But perhaps there was nothing left to do since the heavens, the earth, and all their hosts were completed. So, is it possible that all God could do was rest? I cannot imagine that the all-knowing all-powerful God was actually tired since He mostly spoke creatively, with one instance of physical exertion accounted for in Genesis 2:7. And if He has all power and is all powerful, why would He even need to rest? Or surely since He is all-knowing, He would have known to pace Himself significantly better and not overexert Himself from all the speaking He did, so there would be no need to rest!

However, the text does not indicate that He was tired; it simply states He rested from all the work He performed and completed. This implies that regardless of the level of effort extended or the type of effort given, everything He did in chapter 1 was considered work. So after it was done, He rested. This is the first mention of the concept of rest, and it is introduced as an occurrence because of work being performed. And it also occurred as a result of the work completed. God rested from the completion of His work. God rested. God took time to stop and rest. We do not know if He was tired or sleepy, but He rested at a specific time, after a specific point, and for a specific reason.

Hustle & Bustle

God's actions contrast with the world we live in today, which is a whirlwind of activity, movement, and busyness. So many people struggle to make ends meet; they may need to work two or three jobs to support their families, pay their bills, or to simply put food on the table. Others, like myself, work in corporate environments where the workload and demands are so heavy that they end up working sixty-plus hours a week, six to seven days a week.

In either scenario, most often the work is performed at the expense of our personal well-being. This is just one side of the equation. There are still the daily tasks of maintaining one's household, whether it's cleaning, doing repairs, washing clothes, preparing and cooking meals, grocery shopping, taking kids to school, helping children with homework, or chauffeuring teens between activities. Regardless of the category, there are still a number of other things to do after paid work is over.

Unlike many other countries, several American companies still offer minimal personal time off or holiday time. For example, for the nearly ten years that I lived and worked in the Caribbean, most companies provided at least four weeks of vacation time that did not include holidays or sick time—those were offered separately. One company I worked for even offered thirty sick days regardless of staff level, and those days were available from the first day of employment. In time, these policies changed because many people took advantage and abused the company's good will.

On the other hand, I also know people whose companies offer only ten personal days per year. This is despite their working hectic, grueling schedules or constantly being on call. Statistics show that employees in the United States are generally less productive and less happy than employees in some other countries due to the lack of work-life balance. People who work with more balance tend to be more productive as well as more content with their lives.

Rest is used in various contexts in Scripture, but in Genesis, as per the Hebrew, תבש, šā·āaā, at its core root it means to cease or desist from labor.[4] Similarly, Merriam-Webster defines rest as follows: "a bodily state characterized by minimal functional and metabolic activities; freedom from activity or labor; a state of motionlessness or inactivity; peace of mind or spirit."[5]

Both definitions align in that God ceased His activities and took the time to chill out!

Good Blessed and Sanctified

Now in all the days prior to the seventh day, the text describes how for nearly all the creative activities He performed, God saw that each was good, or He called them good. But on the seventh day when He rested, God did something more than just declare the day was good: "Then God blessed the seventh day and sanctified it. . . ." He did two more things—He blessed the seventh day and sanctified it.

---

4 R. Laird Harris, Gleason L. Archer, Jr., and Bruce K. Waltke, eds., *Theological Wordbook of the Old Testament* (TWOT) (Chicago: Moody Press, 1980), 902, entry 2323.

5 *Merriam*-Webster, s.v. "rest (*n.*)," https://www.merriam-webster.com/dictionary/rest.

This contrasts with the other blessings God gave in chapter 1. In Genesis 1:22, He blessed the living creatures and told them to "be fruitful and multiply." In Genesis 1:28, again we see God blessing living creatures, this time male and female. He repeats the same message and tells them to "be fruitful and multiply." However, in the third blessing the object is not someone but something. And this time instead of the complement to the blessing being "be fruitful and multiply," it is sanctified.

In this context for each instance where He gave His blessing, God also gave a direction for multiplication. He gave His approval for what was made and said for them to multiply and continue the creative work through productivity and fruitfulness. Although the seventh day is not a living thing, God sanctifying it implies the same process of multiplication and fruitfulness as in blessing the seventh day; He was blessing the cyclical pattern of the seventh day. Therefore, it was not a one-time blessing, but a recurring pattern of blessing that He established starting with Himself for His creation to subsequently and continuously partake on a recurring basis. A time exists for everything—there is a time for work and a time for rest. God took time to rest after the time He worked.

Although the completion of the work was the time when God took His rest, this was not the trigger for when rest should occur. He blessed the seventh day itself, so it is the day of rest that is blessed. This sets the precedent for the recurring time cycle of rest on a go-forward basis.

———

Work is good, but rest is blessed.

———

He called the day or time of rest blessed, which implies that to rest is a blessing from God. He provides a payoff for work that is done and labor completed. It could be inferred if rest is not taken, the blessing of God cannot be experienced. God demonstrated this key principle when He rested, which emphasizes its importance and sets the tone for its progression as a required practice in subsequent Scripture.

According to Jon Oswalt's definition of the word *blessing*, הכרב, (*bᵉ·rākâ*), in the *Theological Wordbook of the Old Testament* (TWOT):

> In general, the blessing is transmitted from the greater to the lesser. . . . Its major function seems to have been to confer abundant and effective life upon something . . . or someone. The verbal blessing . . . was normally futuristic. However, it could be descriptive, an acknowledgment that the person addressed was evidently possessed of this power for abundant and effective living.[6]

It directly implies that there is a benefit to be gained in rest. God blessed rest and the time for rest so that the person who rests is empowered to live abundantly and effectively. He provides assurance for repose and freedom from activity or labor.

Rest is ordained by God. Rest is a blessing from God.

Not only did God bless the day, He also sanctified the day. Generally, to sanctify means to set apart. He sets aside a distinctive

6 TWOT, 132, entry 285.

time for rest, a time to stop working or a time to do nothing once the work is completed. It is a time that God dedicated and consecrated. This is interesting as even in the description of His creation of male and female, the word "sanctified" is not used, although He blessed them. Instead, it is referenced to the seventh day and suggests a cause-effect link that classifies the day as sanctified. He called it sanctified because in the seventh day He rested from all the work He created and made.

Thus, while God was working and performing all His creative activity, none of those were considered as set apart. But the day of rest, the day He was not busy, when He was not consumed with work with tasks and doings, is the day He set aside to bless, sanctify, and dedicate as a special day from the other days of the week.

Sanctify—to set apart, to distinguish, and to dedicate.

From a biblical perspective, one day was set aside for rest versus six days for work. So does that mean significantly fewer days are needed for rest, that just one day of rest is enough to make up for six days given for work? As we continue to progress, Scripture shows that God offers respite beyond one day a week. Rest is ordained by God. Rest is a blessing from God.

Some Play

I remember the first time I traveled "down under." A friend of mine moved to Australia, and I decided to visit her. Given the distance, I thought it made sense to travel to other countries in that area, so I included New Zealand and Fiji on my itinerary. Over the next year, I creatively found every opportunity to earn miles and acquired enough miles to fly business class round-trip on Qantas Airlines using the miles I earned (which is exceptionally rare). An airline agent was kind enough to tell me when to call and reserve.

Although I rejoiced in the luxury of my seat, which converted into a 180-degree flat bed with private cabin service, I still could not relax. It was definitely the favor of the Lord, who blessed me with plane tickets that typically cost several thousands of dollars for less than $300. He blessed me with a fantastic eighteen-day trip, but still I could not relax on the plane due to anxiety (truth be told, a fear of flying). Even though I stretched out on the flat plane bed wearing my Qantas pajama set with matching Qantas socks and sleep mask (can you tell I am a fan of Qantas?), I still could not sleep. Despite the six-hour flight from New York to Los Angeles, with a nearly all-day layover in Los Angeles, I spent most of the fourteen-hour flight to New Zealand tossing and turning. Every time we hit turbulence, I would jump up praying (quietly—sometimes loudly), and glaring at everyone who dared not to call on the name of God too. My fear did not allow the truth of God's goodness to register. Instead, it overshadowed my ability to savor God's favor—He had tremendously blessed me to take the trip and thus would protect me throughout my journey.

My inability to sleep or rest well on an international flight, while on vacation, can in no way compare to the great difficulty many people experience from acute insomnia or chronic sleep disorders. But sometimes we think we can keep going and going and discount the need for rest, and think it is OK to continue down that path. Sometimes we become so busy that we are unable to see what is really important. As Christians we are not exempt. We take on too many things. We make too many commitments and overextend ourselves. Sometimes the churches we attend or ministries we serve exacerbate the problem by using submission and obedience as a means to push and pull for more of our time.

Consider this: are all your obligations necessary or are they inadvertently impacting your family, health, personal well-being, and most importantly, your spiritual walk? A constant competition occurs for your time between family, work, church, and just everyday life.

Simply put, the principle of rest is not being applied in our lives. Because the principle was originally attached to a seventh-day requirement in the Old Testament, it is not consistently practiced, as it is most often falsely assumed to be extraneous. However, although rest is established in the Old Testament, that does not negate its relevance and applicability as a principle that still works today.

Reflect

* *Are you all work and no play?*

* *Are all the activities you are involved in needed and required?*

* *Are you managing your time in such a way that important activities like time with God, family, and self are included in your daily and weekly schedule?*

* *How much time do you take each week to rest?*

Response

Respond and journal how each of the key principles below applies to you.

* *Creative power to speak forth structure from chaos, fruit from barrenness, and light from darkness.*

* *A time and a season exist for everything—there is a time for work and a time for rest.*

* *Work is good, but rest is blessed.*

* *Rest is ordained by God. Rest is a blessing from God.*

* *Sanctify—to set apart, to distinguish, and to dedicate.*

Rest

"Then God blessed the seventh day and sanctified it, because in it. He rested from all His work which God had created and made."

Genesis 2:3

Lord, thank you for sanctifying me. Reveal anything in me that hinders me from being set apart. Teach me appropriate time management and project management so that I can steward the affairs of my life effectively. Give me wisdom of how to lead my household, while at times managing competing priorities across my family, spiritual walk, work, ministry, and personal needs.

CHAPTER THREE

Are You in the Right Bed?

WHEN I PLANNED MY FIRST TRIP TO ASIA, I wanted to maximize the time by juggling my allotted vacation days with needed travel time. Considering it would take almost twenty-four hours to get there, in addition to crossing the international dateline, it meant I would lose three vacation days for the travel on flights to and from the States.

Well, being smart, I assumed I would sleep on the flight back and return to work the day I arrived. Considering the flight was sixteen hours long, I thought I would sleep a good chunk of that time and be well rested for work. Assumptions are not always good, especially when you already know that you are a horrible flyer and rarely sleep on planes due to sheer panic at the slightest hint of turbulence. So, after an awesome trip traipsing around Hong Kong, Singapore, Malaysia, and Bali, where God protected and covered us by plane, bus, taxi, and train, everything went as scheduled in my handy Excel spread-sheet plan—almost.

I did not factor in jet lag upon my return. I did not factor in how the lack of rest and sleep would significantly impact my going back to work straight from the airport. I erroneously assumed a sixteen-hour flight would make me want to sleep. Since my body had adapted to the Asian time zone due to the length of the trip, I hardly slept on the flight. And it was too late to request more days. And it wasn't appropriate to request sick days immediately following personal time off.

If you have ever experienced jet lag, then you know it is no joke. I absolutely could not keep my eyes open. I would take breaks at work and go to the parking lot and nap in my car. A few times while driving on the highway, I had to pull over to shake myself from sleep to not cause an accident. One of the places I slept a few times for quick naps (one time it lasted almost two hours) was in one of my workplace's wellness rooms. *Wellness* was the politically correct term, but it was really a lactation room. When I saw the room had a reclining lounger, I knew it was pre-ordained just for me. Since I needed wellness, I used it for my jet-lag sickness. God knows my heart.

Although the room locked from the inside, I could never relax; I repeatedly woke up and was always nervous someone would somehow walk in. Furthermore, it was extremely bright with fluorescent lighting that wasn't conducive to my wellness purpose. None of these places were the right place to rest.

A New Bed

The Israelites in the Old Testament were a people who needed the right place to rest. They were the seed of Abraham, whom God chose and blessed. He also promised Abraham He would bless his seed (Genesis 12, 17). Yet even though Abraham's seed was blessed, over time they ended up enslaved to another nation for over 400 years. Many would consider this not much of a blessing, but this is not a discussion about the sociology of that period. Abraham's descendants cried out to God for help and deliverance from their enslavement. Based on His covenant with Abraham, God took them as His own and entered a covenant with them. He promised to love them and watch over them if they would in turn trust and serve Him as their God.

God delivered them from their bondage and established them as an independent nation. As a new nation, God outlined laws and standards for them to follow. The directives served to provide them structure and guidance. He started the process with a base set of ten commandments (Exodus 20), which served as the core foundation from which all other stipulations would follow.

In Exodus, God takes the next step to set out a detailed framework that outlines the mechanics of how the seventh day should be practiced. The Genesis account primarily focuses on what God did, but a transition happens in Exodus where the focus is no longer on what God did but on what He requires from the Israelites. It calls for obedience from those who are in a relationship with Him.

A key test of covenant obedience occurred when the Israelites realized they no longer had ready access to food, as they did when they were slaves. But God provided them food daily. They only needed to collect it every day for six days a week. He instructed that they collect twice the amount on the sixth day to make up for not going out on the seventh day to collect:

Now on the sixth day they gathered twice as much bread, two omers for each one. When all the leaders of the congregation came and told Moses, then he said to them, "This is what the Lord meant: Tomorrow is a Sabbath observance, a holy Sabbath to the Lord. Bake what you will bake and boil what you will boil, and all that is left over put aside to be kept until morning." So they put it aside until morning, as Moses had ordered, and it did not become foul nor was there any worm in it. Moses said, "Eat it today, for today is a Sabbath to the Lord; today you will not find it in the field. Six days you shall gather it, but on the seventh day, the Sabbath, there will be none." It came about on the seventh day that some of the people went out to gather, but they found none. Then the Lord said to Moses, "How long do you refuse to keep My commandments and My instructions? See, the Lord has given you the Sabbath; therefore He gives you bread for two days on the sixth day. Remain every man in his place; let no man go out of his place on the seventh day." So the people rested on the seventh day" (Exodus 16:22–30).

———

Obedience to God involves trust—that He will protect,
provide for, heal, strengthen, comfort, and cover you.

———

As in the Genesis account, the people were to work six days and on the sixth day perform extra work in anticipation that no work would be done on the seventh day. Verse 30 says, "So the people rested on the seventh day." The ability to trust was in play: (a) would they trust God enough to obey, and (b) would they trust God to provide?

The ability to trust God was needed. Could the people trust God enough not to work every day but still provide to meet their needs for the seventh day? Could they trust God enough to only work their land for six years, and every seventh year let it rest while believing that God would meet their needs for the entire year? Well, considering the other option was to be stoned to death, I am thinking it was a law worth learning! How about you: do you trust God enough to obey Him? Do you trust that He will provide?

Ancient Hebrews generally thrived or failed according to the effort of their hands, doing work such as farming or shepherding. If you did not work, you would not eat. Thus, a feeling of self-reliance could prevail, where they believed their productivity and fruitfulness was based on their own effort. However, God wanted them to rely on Him as their covenant God.

———

Do you trust God enough to obey Him?
Do you trust Him enough to provide?

———

When He entered covenant with them and gave them the commandments, it was not due to His being some type of controlling chauvinist who got kicks out of bullying people around and telling them what to do. Instead, He created a system for them to follow in order to draw them to Him, and He in turn would cover them in fidelity, faithfulness, and love.

The premise of the Sabbath develops further throughout Exodus. It becomes not only a test of the people's ability to walk in God's instruction (Exodus 16:4), but also part of God's guiding law as the fourth commandment. The commandment reads as follows:

Remember the Sabbath day, to keep it holy. Six days you shall labor and do all your work, but the seventh day is a

Sabbath of the Lord your God; in it you shall not do any work, you or your son or your daughter, your male or your female servant or your cattle or your sojourner who stays with you. For in six days the Lord made the heavens and the earth, the sea and all that is in them, and rested on the seventh day; therefore the Lord blessed the Sabbath day and made it holy (Exodus 20:8–11).

Interestingly, this commandment precedes other ones in its importance, such as honor one's parents, do not murder, do not commit adultery, and do not steal.

Lawful Rest

On the other hand, the fourth commandment immediately follows commandments that refer to the acknowledgment of the sovereignty of God, His position in our worship of Him and how we reverence Him. The fourth commandment comes across almost as a hinge between the first three commandments and the remaining six. The first four commandments mainly relate directly to God, whereas commandments five through ten directly address conditions related to general conduct and morality. This emphasis highlights observance of the Sabbath as not just a regular day but a day set aside with symbolic meaning, reverence, and value. The severity for anyone who violated the command was punishable by death (Exodus 31:14; Numbers 15:32–36).

Additionally, most of the commandments are written as negative directives preceded by the phrase "You shall not." Only two commandments are written affirmatively, where it says what one should do: (1) remember the Sabbath day (v. 4) and (2) honor your father and your mother (v. 12). These commandments describe what God wants the Israelites to do. Each describes a command for the people to respect and honor something or someone. All nations and countries have laws, so it is not unusual that God provided Israel with the same. However, one key distinction is that God created the Sabbath as a designated time of worship for His people to proactively discipline themselves away from the normality of their daily activities and work, to rest and reflect on God. The time was deemed so important that He set the precedent for the seventh day, put it into law, and death was the punishment for any person who did not comply. He set aside, i.e., sanctified, the Sabbath, which made it holy.

Professor Thomas McComiskey's explanation for sanctification corroborates this premise:

> A basic element of Israelite religion was the maintenance of an inviolable distinction between the spheres of the sacred and the common or profane (Numbers 18:32). That which was inherently holy or designated so by divine decree or cultic rite was not to be treated as common. The Sabbath was holy, and the restrictions connected with that day served to maintain its distinctive nature and to guard against its being treated as common. That which was dedicated to God was conceived of as entering the sphere of the "holy." [7]

Additionally, what is also slightly different in the Exodus passage from the Genesis verse is the command itself relates to "remembering the Sabbath" (v8).

---

7 TWOT, 787, entry 1990.

Exodus 31:13–17 provides more insight about what and why they should remember the Sabbath.

> But as for you, speak to the sons of Israel, saying, 'You shall surely observe My Sabbaths; for this is a sign between Me and you throughout your generations, that you may know that I am the Lord who sanctifies you. Therefore you are to observe the Sabbath, for it is holy to you. Everyone who profanes it shall surely be put to death; for whoever does any work on it, that person shall be cut off from among his people. For six days work may be done, but on the seventh day there is a Sabbath of complete rest, holy to the Lord; whoever does any work on the Sabbath day shall surely be put to death. So the sons of Israel shall observe the Sabbath, to celebrate the Sabbath throughout their generations as a perpetual covenant.' It is a sign between Me and the sons of Israel forever; for in six days the Lord made heaven and earth, but on the seventh day He ceased from labor, and was refreshed.

To remember the Sabbath meant to honor it by observing and following it.

The Right Place of Rest

My siblings and I attempt to take a trip together every year with our parents. Sometimes we are successful and sometimes we're not. One successful year we all agreed to take a Caribbean cruise. We all flew from Chicago to Puerto Rico, where we would board the cruise ship. Surprisingly, even though Puerto Rico is a US territory, there are not many nonstop flights from Chicago to Puerto Rico, so we had to take a connecting flight. Because we live on the edge, instead of flying a day early and booking a hotel for one night, we all flew the same day we were to board the ship. Hence, we all had to leave our homes in the middle of the night to catch extremely early flights to ensure our connecting flights arrived in time to board the ship.

If you have ever been on a cruise ship, not only do you typically travel to a different location to get on the ship but waiting to board the ship can also be a lengthy endeavor. Most often, your room may not be available upon arrival, so you putter around until it is ready. Fortunately, my room, which I was sharing with my sister, was available. My nephew chose to stay in our room instead of being under his parents' watchful eyes. He was due to sleep on the overhead bed, but housekeeping had yet to set it up when we finally made it back to the room. So after our pre-crack-of-dawn departure, standing in the forever line to board the ship, and overindulgent eating to make up for all the meals we missed while traveling, my sister and I decided to rest before we went to dinner.

Our room was the size of a large closet. And while my sister and I could lie down on top of our individual twin-sized beds that were more like camping cots loaded with pillows to make them look better than they actually were, my nephew sat on the corner of my bed looking miserable. The next thing I knew, he stretched his 6'4," 250-pound plus frame on my bed with his head at the opposite end of the bed from my head. I was nearly conked out and too tired to protest.

But at some point, we heard a thunderous boom and were jarred awake in fright, which quickly turned to hysterical laughter at the sight of my nephew looking completely confused and dazed on the floor after falling off the bed. Regardless of how gingerly he tried to stretch out his football player–like frame parallel to my 5'2" blessed frame, the cot-sized bed could not hold us both. Needless to say, it was not the right place for him to rest.

God desires for His people to be in the right place of covenant relationship with Him, which is why He took so much extensive time and effort to outline in detail structure and boundaries. It was not supposed to be a place of restriction but a place whereby they acknowledged His reign over them as a newly established nation. The Sabbath was not just a day of rest to cease from work; it also symbolized a covenant relationship between God and His people. When it was observed, it demonstrated that God's people were committed and loyal to Him due to their reverence of Him.

It was a day also set aside as a sign to remember the works of God. To remember something involves bringing it to mind and thinking about it. To remember can include reflection or meditation. It was a day of rest, but also a day to remember the works of God and celebrate being refreshed and re-energized for the upcoming week. And it was required not only for people. Everything pertaining to a person's household was supposed to rest—servants, guests, animals, and even one's land so that all could be refreshed (Exodus 23:10–12).

A time of rest involves reflection, remembrance, and celebration.

R & R

Remembrance & Reverence. Further still in Deuteronomy 5, another reason for rest is provided—reverence. He wanted the Israelites to not only remember but to reverence God. It was a time for them to cease from labor to rest and remember the works of God on the Sabbath. It reflected an act of worship and reverence to God. Deuteronomy 5:12, 15 says:

Observe the Sabbath day to keep it holy, as the Lord your God commanded you. . . . You shall remember that you were a slave in the land of Egypt, and the Lord your God brought you out of there by a mighty hand and by an outstretched arm; therefore the Lord your God commanded you to observe the Sabbath day.

The Sabbath was a day for the people to remember the creative works of God over the earth. It stressed His sovereignty and majesty. It was a day to remember the works of God and how He delivered them and set them free. It highlights His closeness—His capacity to hear their cry in the depth of their pain and despair—that He is still yet close enough to stretch out His arm and grab you with His hand from the pit of darkness, bondage, and hopelessness.

In the Sabbath is rest, which is the blessing of God, and refreshment. It is observed, but it is also a place to be—a place of rest where we remember and acknowledge God. It is a place where we do not focus on work, family obligations, property, or other types of distractions, but it is a time where we rest and free ourselves from the strife of life, if only for a day. To observe the Sabbath is to rest in God. If we do not take or specifically set aside time that is uninhibited with distractions, interruptions, work, phones, social media, ministry, TV, Netflix, Hulu, and so on, when and how can we adequately spend time with God—to reflect on Him, remember His works, and solely spend time with Him and Him alone?

God wants His people to be in a position of rest by practicing a Sabbath rest. You may not practice a literal Sabbath day, but the principle is applicable. He wants our undivided attention in some type of consistent time that we set aside to rest with Him.

Reflect

❋ *Are you in the right place to rest in God?*

❋ *What are the distractions that routinely interrupt your time with God?*

❋ *How could you begin to incorporate a time of Sabbath in your week?*

❋ *What steps do you need to take to discipline your schedule for weekly rest (personal and spiritual)?*

Response

Respond and journal how each of these key principles applies to or impacts you.

❋ *Obedience to God involves trust—that He will protect, provide for, heal, strengthen, comfort, and cover you.*

❋ *I trust God enough to obey Him. I trust Him enough to provide.*

❋ *A time of rest involves reflection, remembrance, and celebration.*

Rest

"So the people rested on the seventh day."

Exodus 16:30

Lord, thank you for the principle of rest. Thank you for showing me the need for it as a spiritual discipline in my life. Teach me how to fully obey you while trusting you to meet all my time management needs: spiritual, family, work, or ministry. Help me to be proactively intentional in taking time to not only rest but to reflect, remember, and celebrate you in a consistent time set aside with you that is free and devoid of all distractions.

CHAPTER FOUR

An Appointed Time

LONG BEFORE ANY OTHER TRANS-ATLANTIC FLIGHT, my very first overseas trip to Europe was a one-week work trip to London, which I met with great excitement and extreme nervousness. The sheer thought of flying over the ocean for several hours at one time caused me to hyperventilate every time I thought about it. While I prepared and planned all the places I wanted to see, I was extremely anxious. I even asked my pastor at the time to join me at the airport on the day of departure to keep me company until the flight departed—and of course to pray with me. Thankfully, we were good friends, and he indulged my feeble faith. We prayed before my departure, and I finally grabbed on to some confidence to stop hyperventilating as I boarded the plane.

The Lord gave me peace on the overnight flight, but I did not sleep for even one second. Upon arrival, my colleague and I showered (separately of course) in the business lounge and took a two-hour train ride to the client's office. I think the excitement and adrenaline of being in London helped me to work the entire day and even go for dinner with the client without needing to sleep earlier. By the time I reached my hotel room, I was ready to crash after being awake for over twenty-four hours.

I did not know the importance of using the hotel wake-up call combined with my cell phone alarm. I am not sure what made me think I could rely on my normal internal 6:00 a.m. alarm clock from a different time zone. Total failure. I honestly feel it was God that eventually woke me. I slept through my cell phone alarm, and the battery on my internal alarm completely malfunctioned. I had over a dozen missed calls from my colleague, whom I reported to on the project. I would miss the morning client meeting. I invented a story of being ill and found my way to the client's office. God knows my heart. In that moment, I felt completely sick from lack of sleep and disorientation, and a bit nervous about what the client would say about my missing the meeting I was supposed to lead.

There is an appointed time for everything.

It all worked out, and they were gracious—thank God—or maybe it was just British cultural politeness? On another note, I still cannot understand why my colleague did not just call the hotel room versus only my cell phone. Timing is everything: Time that I should have taken to set up the hotel wake-up call. Time to wake up on time. Time to be at my meeting. There is an appointed time for everything.

Sixes & Sevens

God provided more stipulations about the Sabbath and the practice of it more than any other command. And mostly everything related to it focused on time: six days for work, the seventh day for rest. And as you continue to read through the covenant framework set out through Exodus, Leviticus, Numbers, and Deuteronomy, you will see He adds even more time-related boundaries.

Leviticus 25 describes how God expands the practice of the Sabbath to not just every seventh day but every seventh year. And if that was not the icing on the cake, after the seventh cycle of the seventh year, year forty-nine, they got a back-to-back siesta in the fiftieth year as well—the year of jubilee.

Can you imagine what that would look like today? No—sorry, I cannot come into work today, or for that matter, the entire year. It is my Sabbath year. This would be the law everyone would comply with. It makes me wonder: on every seventh-day Sabbath in the seventh year, did they rest from their rest?

After every six years, the Israelites were required to let their land rest. They were not supposed to sow or gather anything during the seventh year. Leviticus 25:3–7 (AMP) says:

> For six years you shall sow your field, and for six years you shall prune your vineyard and gather in its crop. But in the seventh year there shall be a Sabbath of rest for the land, a Sabbath to the Lord; you shall not sow [seed in] your field nor prune your vineyard. Whatever reseeds itself (uncultivated) in your harvest you shall not reap, nor shall you gather the grapes from your uncultivated vine, it shall be a year of sabbatical rest for the land. And all of you shall have for food whatever the [untilled] land produces during its Sabbath year; yourself, and your male and female slaves, your hired servant, and the foreigners who reside among you, even your domestic animals and the [wild] animals that are in your land shall have all its crops to eat.

Again, we see that their obedience to God would require that they trust Him and that He would provide and sustain them for the entire year from what the untilled land would happen to produce. A three-year time frame would occur with potentially no produce or food to eat. But even in this apparent dilemma, God would provide. He says in Leviticus 25:20–22 (AMP):

> And if you say, "What are we going to eat in the seventh year if we do not sow [seed] or gather in our crops?" then [this is My answer:] I will order My [special] blessing for you in the sixth year, so that it will produce [sufficient] crops for three years. When you are sowing the eighth year, you can still eat old things from the crops, eating the old until the ninth year when its crop comes in.

To be honest, this comes across as bizarre to me. Why did they have to go through this recurrent process every seven years? Was the test of their obedience already not enough every seven days and now they also needed to be tested for an entire year every seven years? What lesson did God want to teach them? And why did it have to be every seven years? How come it was not ten? Or even fifteen?

Without delving into the intricacies of farming or agriculture, or the benefits of land fallowing, a key observation I noted is God's extreme care with timing and seasons. Given the care He provides in the guidance for the Israelites to follow, they had little room for uncertainty and misunderstanding as each season and time is specifically and clearly explained. Like clockwork, they knew exactly when they were supposed to rest and when to work. And everyone and everything related to each household rested, including their land, guests, and animals.

Jubilee Rest

The recurring seven cycles of seven years led to the fiftieth year—designated their jubilee year. Although at first glance the rules the Israelites needed to follow look onerous, as well as the fortitude of trust they needed to build in God, their obedience was not God's only concern. God demonstrates His overarching love for the Israelites not only in His provision toward them but also in His active care for their well-being. In addition to His divine sustenance and provision through year seven and through year one in the restart of the seven-year cycle, the Israelites never lacked. Their obedience secured the blessings and favor of God.

———

Obedience to God always brings blessings and favor.

———

The jubilee year reflected God's divine providence and engagement in their ongoing freedom, prosperity, and overall fortune. In addition to the recurring theme of the Sabbath rest, the jubilee year also provided two other key benefits to the Israelites: restitution of property and proclamation of release.

First, the restitution law allowed for personal property and land to be returned to its owner in the jubilee year. It included a law of redemption by which Israelites could buy back their land or redeem it with specific provisions if they had been forced to sell it previously (Leviticus 25:24–28). The priests or Levites would have permanent redemption rights. The jubilee year provided an opportunity for everyone to be restored with whatever they might have lost during the prior seasons. They could be put back into a position of balance from any situation that did not benefit them during the sowing seasons. Anything lost or unjustly taken was to be returned to the rightful owner, in addition to compensation for any related injury or loss.

This law of restitution closely resembles the principle of restoration that God desires for His people today. He is not an autocratic czar that only seeks and demands our obedience. The framework of obedience He outlined for the Israelites fostered humility and submission to God to rely on His sovereignty. His sovereign rule over His people differs distinctively from that of the Egyptians, who held the Israelites captive and were abusive, unjust, and evil in their dealings. God rules His people with justice, fairness, and love, and He is empathetic to the needs and plights of His people.

When we obey God's rule over us, we humble ourselves before Him and submit to His way. And while He does require obedience, most fundamental is that He covers, protects, and blesses His people based on our obedience. The law detailed the applicability and practice of restitution and restoration to the Israelites' friends, family, foreigners, slaves, and guests alike. No partiality occurred in its execution. In the fidelity that He extends toward us, likewise, God expects us to treat each other with fidelity and justice.

Second, the fiftieth Sabbath year was a year of release. It was a year that all Israelites could be released from any type of servitude or hired worked arrangement. As the people of God, they were no longer subject to enslavement. God intended and desired for them to remain free. However, if happenstance caused them to be bound to anyone, the jubilee year released them from any such arrangements going forward. The law said, "Because the Israelites are my servants, whom I brought out of Egypt, they must not be sold as slaves. Do not rule over them ruthlessly but fear your God" (Leviticus 25:42–43). His covenant with them was based on freedom.

Not Bedtime but Rest Time

God is a God of covenant. He honors relationship. When you are in a relationship with Him, your cries and groaning do not go unheard. He hears your anguish; He sees your pain. His responsiveness to the Israelites reflects His nature and character to those with whom He is connected. Exodus 6:5–8 says:

> Moreover, I have heard the groaning of the Israelites, whom the Egyptians are enslaving, and I have remembered my covenant. Therefore, say to the Israelites: "I am the Lord, and I will bring you out from under the yoke of the Egyptians. I will free you from being slaves to them, and I will redeem you with an outstretched arm and with mighty acts of judgment. I will take you as my own people, and I will be your God. Then you will know that I am the Lord your God, who brought you out from under the yoke of the Egyptians."

God is a God of freedom, and He wants to free you from whatever yokes of slavery or bondage you are embroiled in. He wants to release you from the layers of restrictions from your past—past sins, past hurts, past abuse. He wants to release you from the limitations of your environment, whether its institutionalized systems of inequity, racism, classism, or economic injustice. He wants to release you from the confines of your culture and past experiences that shape how you think, act, and behave—anything that limits you from experiencing full liberty in Him.

God wants to release you from whatever binds you, to a release in Him. He did not just free the Israelites from slavery and leave them, but He provided a framework and a path, as well as guidance, which they could follow into their freedom. It will not always be a struggle, always laborious, always sowing and never reaping.

God wants to release you into jubilee—an appointed time consecrated for restitution, restoration, release, and rest in Him. Unlike the Israelites, you don't have to wait for a literal fifty years. God says that now—today—is the appointed time for the favor of the Lord for you, for the ones who walked in disciplined obedience even when it was uncomfortable. He brings good news with the anointing that breaks the yoke of debt, sickness, bondage, and fear. He brings breakthrough and victory in time of jubilee.

Leviticus 25:10 says, "Consecrate the fiftieth year and proclaim liberty throughout the land to all its inhabitants. It shall be a jubilee for you. . . ." The jubilee had to be announced and proclaimed. At the appointed time, the Israelites had to initiate their jubilee through proclamation. The jubilee provided their reset button where they were no longer bound by poor decisions or financial downturn but restored to a new path for reaping, blessings, and flowing.

———

God releases, restores, and resets.

———

After my epiphany on the lack of rest in my life, in addition to the other changes I made, I also incorporated a Sabbath into my week. Without getting into a theological debate on the right day, I decided to practice the Sabbath in my life by choosing a day of the week where I would not work. My practice of this principle is not perfect. It is a work in progress, but it definitely has been effective since I started.

God knows what He is doing. Herein lies the problem—we can choose to take time off from our day job, but then there may be a host of other tasks on our plates, such as household chores, familial obligations, ministry work, and so on. All of these put a demand on our time, to a point where we still end up not completely shutting off. While all those things still need to be done, unfortunately they still constitute work. It is difficult to completely shut down to a point where we avoid doing much of anything. However, since God ordained rest, to do so must be worth it. I continue to strive to achieve this on a consistent basis.

Secular research even emphasizes the benefits of taking a break from all work. The benefits include

- the ability to mentally relax, i.e., to woos-ah.

- time to refresh ourselves emotionally.

- the opportunity to reflect on what we did, what we need to do, and where we need to go.

- focused and attentive time with God without distractions, rambling thoughts, or pressure to get started on work.

- to get a good night's sleep that allows us to physically restore.

Each of these align with benefits scientists specify too. For example, in an article published in *INC* magazine, credence is given for religions' principle of rest. "A Day of Rest: 12 Scientific Reasons It

Works" by Rhett Power espouses twelve reasons, based on science, that rest works:[8]

1. Time out reduces stress.

2. Time out gives you a chance to move.

3. Completely divesting from your work on a regular basis reduces inflammation and the risk of heart disease.

4. Getting away from work boosts your immune system.

5. Speaking of sleep, you'll do it better during time out of work.

6. Your active time off adds years to your life.

7. Taking regular time away from work restores mental energy.

8. When you take out time for yourself, you're more creative.

9. You're also more productive when you take time out from work.

10. You'll focus better at work if you take your weekly reju- venation time.

---

8 Rhett Powers, "A Day of Rest: 12 Scientific Reasons It Works," Inc., January 1, 2017, https://www.inc.com/rhett-power/a-day-of-rest-12-scientific-reasons-it-works.html.

11. Your day off improves your short-term memory.

12. With regular time away from work, you might even love your job again.

We need to intentionally seek rest on a regular basis. There will always be things to do and reasons we should not stop working, but ultimately, the benefits to recharge, refresh, and reset always greatly outweigh the costs.

An appointed time exists for your blessing—when time collides with the doors of opportunity God wills for you. Ecclesiastes is one of my favorite books of the Bible. Ecclesiastes 3:9–15 says:

What profit is there to the worker from that in which he toils. I have seen the task which God has given the sons of men with which to occupy themselves. He has made everything appropriate in its time. He has also set eternity in their heart, yet so that man will not find out the work which God has done from the beginning even to the end. I know that there is nothing better for them than to rejoice and to do good in one's lifetime; moreover, that every man who eats and drinks sees good in all his labor—it is the gift of God. I know that everything God does will remain forever; there is nothing to add to it and there is nothing to take from it, for God has so worked that men should fear Him. That which is has been already and that which will be has already been, for God seeks what has passed by.

————

*An appointed time exists for your blessing—when time collides
with the doors of the opportunity that God wills for you.*

————

There is good in your labor. There is good in serving God.
There is good in the difficult tests and trials you face, even though
it does not feel like it. God wants you to know that He hears you,
He sees you, and He is present.

Reflect

﹡ *How does your use of time impact your effectiveness and
productivity in your relationship with God? Family? Ministry?
Other areas?*

﹡ *What areas in your life do you need God to restore? Does it include
your relationship with Him?*

﹡ *What areas in your life do you need to walk in freedom? With others?*

Response

Respond and journal how each of the following key principles
applies to or impacts you.

﹡ *There is an appointed time for everything.*

﹡ *Obedience to God always brings blessings and favor.*

* *God releases, restores, and resets.*

* *An appointed time exists for your blessing—when time collides with the doors of the opportunity that God wills for you.*

Rest

". . . proclaim liberty throughout the land to all its inhabitants. It shall be a jubilee for you. . . ."

Leviticus 25:10

I proclaim the favorable year of the Lord in my life. This is the year for increase, blessing, and release. I decree I am free from debt, sickness, bondage, and fear. I release the power of God for breakthrough, victory, deliverance, and faith in my life. I speak divine order over every aspect of my life—family, ministry, business, health, emotions, and spiritual. Chaos, limitation, and confusion must go. Lord, you are my God. I humble myself in submission to obey and follow you all the days of my life. Lord God, be my guide, be my strength, and show me the way you want me to go.

CHAPTER FIVE

Sleep Like a Baby

ONE OF OUR BEST FAMILY VACATIONS WAS A TRIP TO Alaska. I had a bit more flexibility in my schedule, so I decided to go two days ahead of my family and sightsee in Anchorage before they came. I booked an all-day tour that was conducted on a huge coach bus. I did not have a rental car, but the tour provided pick-ups and drop-offs from various attendees' locations. The coach bus picked me up after a few other people, which meant on the return, I would be the last drop-off. It was a great tour. I enjoyed the day and expected my family to arrive by the time I returned to the hotel later that evening.

Apparently, after the tour ended and the driver commenced passenger drop-offs, I dozed off, not into a light sleep but a deep sleep. I skipped the rapid eye movement (REM) stage, which is somewhere in between. Again, I honestly felt it was God that jarred me awake as I immediately noted the following upon opening my eyes: it was completely dark outside; I was the only person on the bus, which was parked in the middle of the bus depot, with hundreds of other buses parked for the night; I had no cell phone signal; the bus door was closed; and the driver was walking away from the bus. Thankfully, adrenaline kicked in and I started banging on the window and calling—well, yelling—for the driver to return. (And also wondering what kind of driver just leaves their bus without performing a complete walkthrough before exiting!)

I could tell she was shocked and confused as she came back to the bus. Right then I was struck with a healthy dose of the giggles and could not stop laughing as I begged her to take me back to my hotel, which was across town. Finally, she obliged (once the Lord answered my silent prayer to help me stop laughing, so she did not think I was a lunatic who purposely hid on the bus). Otherwise, I would have been stuck in a bus depot overnight thousands of miles away from home with no cell phone signal. I could tell that she did not find my barely suppressed and muffled laughter amusing as she drove back across town. I did give her a nice tip for her trouble.

Within our human ability, we will always miss the mark following the law and will never achieve the rest of God. The Old Testament law was a precursor to what God wanted to fulfill through Jesus. The law pointed the way for relationship with the divine and the importance of obedience to God. However, complying with the law also involved a great deal of legalistic effort and more of a burden to remember every ordinance and statute. But the New Testament, through Jesus, would provide a complete path for resting in God.

Out with the Old, In with the New

Throughout the Israelites' history, they disobeyed God recurrently and routinely failed to meet their part of the covenant relationship with Him. Despite their constantly breaking the covenant, God did not abandon them. Instead, with His outstretched arm, He still sent His Son in time to serve as a mediator and a repairer of the breach between them. This was to restore His relationship not only with the Israelites but with all humankind.

Isaiah prophesied of this. Isaiah 61:1–3, 7–8 highlight God's intention for the reestablishment of a covenant that supersedes all those that came prior.

> The Spirit of the Lord God is upon me, Because the Lord has anointed me To bring good news to the afflicted; He has sent me to bind up the brokenhearted, To proclaim liberty to captives And freedom to prisoners; To proclaim the favorable year of the Lord And the day of vengeance of our God; To comfort all who mourn, To grant those who mourn in Zion, Giving them a garland instead of ashes, The oil of gladness instead of mourning, The mantle of praise instead of a spirit of fainting. So they will be called oaks of righteousness, The planting of the Lord, that He may be glorified. . . . Instead of your shame you will have a double portion, And instead of humiliation they will shout for joy over their portion. Therefore they will possess a double portion in their land, Everlasting joy will be theirs. For I, the Lord, love justice, I hate robbery in the burnt offering; And I will faithfully give them their recompense And make an everlasting covenant with them.

This new covenant would no longer be based on keeping the law; instead, it would be based on acceptance and authentic love of God through belief in His Son, who provides a way of escape from the bondage of sin and the systems of this world.

The prophecy declared in Isaiah sees its fulfillment in the New Testament. Hereafter, a shift occurs from the Old to the New Testament. The New Testament expands the meaning of rest to include the fulfillment of spiritual rest in God. The two are still intricately connected, as the physical rest previously described provided the opportunity to remember and reflect on the things God performed. The two are now intertwined in the New Testament. The iconic passage that sets the tone for this evolved principle is Matthew 11:28–30:

> Come to Me, all who are weary and heavy-laden, and I will give you rest. Take My yoke upon you and learn from Me, for I am gentle and humble in heart, and you will find rest for your souls. For My yoke is easy and My burden is light.

Instead of compulsory behavior and laws that we are obligated to obey, God gives each of us a cordial invitation to come to Him. In Genesis He told His people to rest. In the New Testament, He invites them to take His rest by coming to Him. Weary and heavy-laden implies more than an exhaustion from physical labor; now it implies mental, social, emotional, and even spiritual fatigue.

The Invite

God invites us to enter a relationship with Him. This invite is provided to all; everyone is given an opportunity to choose Him. He is not a respecter of persons—He does not separate or segregate. Regardless of your gender, class, race, past, or background, He extends His invitation to all.

When God invites us to "come to Him," we make a choice to go His way. First, we respond to His invitation and then we act. He does not force us or make us do anything we do not want to do. We make the decision to accept His invitation, and once we accept it, we move toward God. When we move toward Him, we move toward what He represents and what He offers. In this way, He offers rest.

He is the source of rest. When we accept His invitation and come to Him, it is not conditional or an option—it is a guarantee. Rejecting His invitation indirectly implies that we will not get rest.

When God invites you to come to Him, He invites you to move
toward Him in intimacy—toward His rest.

He says, "I will give you rest." It is personal. Rest from your weariness. Rest from your fatigue. Rest from your stress. Rest from your anxiety. Rest from your burdens. Rest from your fear. Rest from your doubt. Rest from your frustration. Rest from your heaviness. Rest from your past. If you choose to come away from all these things, people, and situations and go to Him, as the source of rest, He will do something different from what you could ever imagine. Rest from your weary hearts. Rest from your tormenting thoughts. Rest from your burdensome labor. He will give you rest. Full stop.

Matthew 11:28–30 shows a cause-effect correlation in that the first part of the passage identifies God as the source: "I" will give you rest. The latter part of the passage highlights the results of going to God, or our part: "you" will find rest. If you go to God, you will find rest. If you go to God, you will find what you need in contrast to what you experience without Him. The rest He gives comes from Him and is in Him. He gives rest in Him and you find rest in Him. In Him you find rest from your weariness and heavy-laden life. He provides spiritual rest and peace, which inevitably influences and impacts you in your environment and how you respond with and to it.

God's invitation to come to Him reflects an active and progressive relationship. He desires a relationship with you, and for you to be near to Him. He desires for you to move toward Him. When you move toward Him, you find rest in Him.

Even with the New Testament's added spiritual implication, rest still means a cease from our labor or striving. But it also expands to include respite that can only be obtained through relationship with God: the evolvement of worship, intimacy, and relationship. In and through Him, God offers life, refreshment, comfort, and peace. Life with Him provides balance. Life in Him provides rest. Life through Him provides harmony.

Life with God provides balance. Life in Him provides rest.
Life through Him provides harmony.

Verse 29 says, "Take my yoke upon you." *Zondervan Encyclopedia* describes a yoke as follows:

A yoke was a piece of timber or a heavy wooden pole, shaped to fit over the neck with curved pieces of wood around

CAN YOU SLEEP LIKE THIS?   67

the neck fastened to the pole, and was used to hitch together a team of draft animals so that they could pull heavy
loads evenly. In the Bible terms are most often used metaphorically to designate a burden, obligation or slavery . . .
and hardships people must bear.[9]

A yoke symbolized submission and is a sign of service. When we
take God's yoke, it means that we are joined and connected to
God. He helps to carry our burdens, and in turn we submit to
serve Him.

God offers something that no other relationship, idol, hobby,
sport, job, or business can provide. Though at times His way is
inexplicable, the nature of His character is always faithful and un-
failing. It is His will to bless, to meet needs, and to fill. However,
the warfare all around us from the aftermath of a global pandemic,
economic recession, civil unrest, unrighteousness, and political
discord can produce an environment of overwhelming uncertainty
and stress that in turn produces weariness and heaviness. But we
do not have to take these yokes upon us.

Jeremiah 31:25 says, "For I satisfy the weary ones and refresh
everyone who languishes." God satisfies, fills, and completes us.
But it is the enemy's desire for us to focus more on the mayhem
of the world around us, in our circumstances, or from the negative
rhetoric from so many voices of influence, be they spiritual, social,
or political. Despite all this, God wants to offer us another way—
His yoke of obedience—which is always balanced with blessing
and reward.

9 Merrill C. Tenney and Moisés Silva, eds., *The Zondervan Encyclopedia of the Bible*
(Zondervan Academic, 2010), vol. 5, 1022.

Like the formless void and darkness over the surface of the deep, the Spirit of God is still moving over the surface of the earth today. He is still present. He is still inviting us into relationship. And He is still inviting us to rest, only now it is not just from our natural labor but to enter an inherent posture of spiritual rest in Him.

So, what hinders us from accepting His invitation to trust in Him, to be confident that not only is He able to carry and bring us through but also that He will? To take up His yoke and way? To learn from Him and His ways? Our yoke and the yokes of others limit and confine us; these burdens inevitably produce weariness. On the other hand, God tells us that His yoke is easy. For many it may not feel easy, but presumably He describes it as easy because we are never alone when we carry it. He is with us as we take up His yoke. He is with us as we bear our burdens through Him. In Him the load is made lighter. He is present with us as we plow through the fields of life.

We are all bombarded with the cares of this life and its demands. At times, the pressure to measure up to the expectations of others can be overwhelming. Our past hurts and disappointments can also cause emotional distress. At times we concede to live in the echoes of our past. A constant battle torments us in our present and weighs down our posture and mind with anxiety and stress. Our responses to the challenges we face are ineffective. We end up in a counterproductive cycle that produces minimal fruit as we are unable to adequately address all our problems. We rely on others, we rely on our job, we rely on our family, we rely on our churches. But how often do we completely rely on God?

We may seek Him, but sometimes our pursuit is lukewarm while we simultaneously and aggressively seek a prophetic word or affirmation from others. We ask Him while we concurrently talk to everyone else to gather perspective and get advice about the best way to handle our issues. We knock on God's door while at the same time pursuing every opportunity to solve and fix our situations independent of Him. We seek quick solutions to try to produce the least amount of pain, resistance, or difficulty.

The Slumber Party

The ability to rest in God first involves a process whereby we take the initiative to move toward Him proactively and steadily. He will not force us to accept Him or His process. I note seven components of this process that transpires between our invitation and acceptance.

1. **Acknowledgment**—We acknowledge our dependence on God. We acknowledge Him as the source of help, refuge, and hope regardless of the noise of the world around us. We recognize that we are helpless without Him. Without Him we do not have the ability to successfully navigate the weight of the burdens of life. Acceptance acknowledges Him as the source of strength.

2. **Submission**—We submit our will to God's way and guidance when we take His yoke. We accept His rule over our life. We bow our self-interests and self-motivations and replace them with His interests and will.

3. **Obedience**—As we practice discipline, we then obey God and comply to the standards He sets out in Scripture and the principles of His character. "For this is the

love of God, that we keep His commandments; and His commandments are not burdensome" (1 John 5:3).

4. **Discipline**—Once we submit to His will, discipline must be practiced in learning and understanding the ways of God. It becomes a disciplined practice of submitting our will, thoughts, and behavior to align to His ways. It is hard to properly take His yoke upon us if we do not know Him, His character, and the extent of His nature. When we do not know Him, it becomes easy to be deceived in believing lies or influenced in contrary patterns of thinking about His character.

5. **Revelation**—When we continue to move toward God in submission and obedience, God progressively reveals Himself and reveals truth to us. The closer we draw to Him, the more He reveals. He reveals more of Himself, more of His wisdom and insight related to our circumstances.

6. **Completion**—We are complete as we rest in God. There is nothing lacking, nothing missing when we rest in Him and His rest is in us. James 1:2–8 says, "Consider it all joy, my brethren, when you encounter various trials, knowing that the testing of your faith produces endurance. And let endurance have its perfect result, so that you may be perfect and complete, lacking in nothing."

———

There is nothing lacking, nothing missing
when we rest in God and His rest is in us.

———

7. **Reward**—Rest is God's reward for us. He blesses us with rest not only physically but also spiritually, mentally, and emotionally. Through our submission and obedience in Him, He provides a path of strength, comfort, and peace. When we move toward Him in an intimate relationship, it facilitates a path to rest and harmony in God.

Rest is ordained by God. Rest is God's reward for you.

In our humanity, it is not normal to consider it joy when we suffer trials and tribulations. The weight of our humanness with its emotions and anxieties, at times can supersede our ability to believe for better or that we will overcome in the face of insurmountable odds. But in God and through His presence, we have the capacity to endure and reach a state of endurance in Him to overcome overwhelming tests. He carries us through our pain, tribulation, and suffering. His presence and grace sustain us during great trials. Consequently, His yoke is easy and His burden light.

Sweet Dreams

We are not left alone to endure or figure things out on our own when we come to God. In our acknowledgment and submission to Him, He gives us guidance, He teaches us, and gives us what we need. God does not trick us or keep us in the dark—He is the way, the truth, and the life. He does not force His way on us but desires for us to choose His way. His nature is gentle. His way is humble. He is low in position, unassuming, and meek, unlike the world. The following scriptures highlight His way:

> **Ephesians 4:20–24**—But you did not learn Christ in this way, if indeed you have heard Him and have been taught in Him, just as truth is in Jesus, that, in reference to your former manner of life, you lay aside the old self, which is being corrupted in accordance with the lusts of deceit, and that you be renewed in the spirit of your mind, and put on the new self, which in the likeness of God has been created in righteousness and holiness of the truth.

> **Jeremiah 6:16**—Thus says the Lord, "Stand by the ways and see and ask for the ancient paths, Where the good way is, and walk in it; And you will find rest for your souls." But they said, "We will not walk in it."

> **1 John 2:4–6**—The one who says, "I have come to know Him," and does not keep His commandments, is a liar, and the truth is not in him; but whoever keeps His word, in him the love of God has truly been perfected. By this we know that we are in Him: the one who says he abides in Him ought himself to walk in the same manner as He walked.

We come to Him, we take His yoke, and we learn from Him: a series of actions that propel us into the heart of God.

Genuine rest comes from a relationship with God. We cannot rest in our own strength or through our own power and proclivities. Real rest comes through a spiritual connection obtainable through intimacy with God. It is a place where we no longer wrestle in our emotions, responses, or thoughts, and we cease from human striving. Instead, we relax. We rest in the hope, character, and Word of God. We rest in Him because we know Him. We rest in Him because we understand His methods. We rest in Him because we recognize His process. We rest in Him because we know His nature. These provide overwhelming evidence for the consistency of His character to do good for us and not evil. It testifies to the consistency of His love towards His children.

Romans 8:31–39 is a wonderful example of this love guarantee.

What then shall we say to these things? If God is for us, who is against us? He who did not spare His own Son, but delivered Him over for us all, how will He not also with Him freely give us all things? Who will bring a charge against God's elect? God is the one who justifies; who is the one who condemns? Christ Jesus is He who died, yes, rather who was raised, who is at the right hand of God, who also intercedes for us. Who will separate us from the love of Christ? Will tribulation, or distress, or persecution, or famine, or nakedness, or peril, or sword? Just as it is written, "For Your sake we are being put to death all day long; We were considered as sheep to be slaughtered." But in all these things we overwhelmingly conquer through Him who loved us. For I am convinced that neither death, nor life, nor angels, nor principalities, nor things present, nor things to come, nor powers, nor height, nor depth, nor any other created thing, will be able to separate us from the love of God, which is in Christ Jesus our Lord.

This is the truth we can possess, despite the noise of the world, the burdens that weigh us, or the testing we face. God is with us and is present in our circumstances.

―――――

God's Word, nature, and process provide overwhelming evidence for
the consistency of His character to do good for you and not evil.

―――――

There is a place of rest God desires for you. It is a place of relationship and intimacy with Him. He wants you to come to Him.
He wants you to follow His way. And He wants you to learn more
of Him. Will you heed His call?

Reflect

* *How will you accept God's invitation and move toward Him in*
relationship and intimacy?

* *What steps will you take to further develop the areas of the process*
that may be lacking or inoperative in your life?

* *Describe the overwhelming evidence of God's goodness and*
faithfulness to you in your life.

Response

Respond and journal how each of the following key principles
applies to or impacts you.

* *When God invites you to come to Him, He invites you to move*
toward Him in intimacy—toward His rest.

* *Life with God provides balance. Life in Him provides rest. Life through Him provides harmony.*

* *There is nothing lacking, nothing missing when we rest in God, and His rest is in us.*

* *Rest is ordained by God. Rest is God's reward for you.*

* *God's Word, nature, and process provide overwhelming evidence for the consistency of His character to do good for you and not evil.*

Rest

"Make me know Your ways, O Lord; Teach me Your paths. Lead me in Your truth and teach me, For You are the God of my salvation; For You I wait all the day. Remember, O Lord, Your compassion and Your lovingkindnesses, For they have been from of old. Do not remember the sins of my youth or my transgressions; According to Your lovingkindness remember me, For Your goodness' sake, O Lord."

Psalm 25:4–8

Lord, I hear you calling me. I repent for where I resisted you and even at times rejected you. Father forgive me for not accepting your invitation. I stand before you now and acknowledge your Lordship. I submit to your call to walk in obedience and discipline to you and your way.

CHAPTER SIX

Who's in Bed with You?

ONE SUMMER I PLANNED A VACATION TO WALES AND Scotland to visit friends in each country, as well as sight-see and tour. After I spent a few days in Wales, I took a train from Wales to Scotland. Depending on the train, this trip can take a minimum of seven hours. I decided to leverage an overnight train so that I would not lose a day of sightseeing. Unfortunately, the train did not leave at a reasonable hour such as 11:00 p.m. or even 1:00 a.m.; it left in the middle of the night around 3:00 a.m., or some other peculiar time in the morning. Given my experience in Alaska, I was determined not to fall asleep and miss my stop in a foreign country, even if the locals did—kind of, sort of—speak English.

As an aside, if you ever hear a Welsh person speak, you will understand—nice, friendly people but definitely a learning curve to understand their dialect. While visiting I had dinner at a friend's house. I always could clearly understand the husband, whom I worked with for a few years; however, I found myself constantly smiling blankly whenever his wife spoke. And then I would turn to him diplomatically for interpretation. I must stress that she was a wonderful host and cooked a lovely meal even if I could not understand most of what she said the entire evening. I digress.

At some point in time on the train ride, I recognized I was fighting a losing battle to not fall asleep. I confirmed with a conductor at least three times the time we were expected to reach my stop. I then set my cell phone alarm for two different times close to my stop's time, along with a vibration just in case I did not hear the alarm. I stuck the phone in my shirt, close to my heart, and proceeded to give in to slumber.

However, after a few hours, I kept feeling a pain in my side but tried to ignore it due to what seemed to be one of the best types of sleep—train sleep. Please try it. Seemingly, I sleep very well on buses and trains, just not on planes.

The pain would not go away. Finally, the intensity and speed of it increased, and my sweet, deep sleep was broken. The lady in the next seat over was severely poking me in my side saying, "Geez, come on." While I was enjoying my rest, my fellow passengers were not. Apparently, they were implying I was making too much noise as I slumbered. Who knew snoring is not limited to a prostrate position?

Sometimes, we accept God's invitation and begin to move closer toward Him, learning from Him and resting in Him. However, many hindrances poke us and keep us from resting consistently in Him. Hebrews 4 directly links the Old Testament concept of rest with the spiritual rest introduced in Matthew. This is explored in the next section.

Wide Awake

Hebrews 4:1–7 says:

> Therefore, let us fear if, while a promise remains of entering
> His rest, any one of you may seem to have come short of it.
> For indeed we have had good news preached to us, just as
> they also; but the word they heard did not profit them, be-
> cause it was not united by faith in those who heard. For we
> who have believed enter that rest, just as He has said, "As I
> swore in My wrath, They shall not enter My rest," although
> His works were finished from the foundation of the world.
> For He has said somewhere concerning the seventh day:
> "And God rested on the seventh day from all His works";
> and again in this passage, "They shall not enter My rest."
> Therefore, since it remains for some to enter it, and those
> who formerly had good news preached to them failed to
> enter because of disobedience, He again fixes a certain day,
> "Today," saying through David after so long a time just as
> has been said before, "Today if you hear His voice, Do not
> harden your hearts."

Hebrews 4 suggests that peril exists for a person who does not
believe, as it subjects one to the wrath of God. The passage quotes
Psalm 95:11: "Therefore I swore in My anger, Truly they shall not
enter into My rest." Psalm 95 speaks of the Lord's dismay at how
the Israelites repeatedly infuriated God in their dismissiveness
and disregard toward Him and the covenant between them. This
treatment occurred despite the fact He mightily delivered them
from slavery and oppression.

Because of the error of their hearts, the Israelites were unable to enter the promised land. The promised land symbolized a place of rest. God called it His rest. It was a place of God's covenant presence and blessing—a place of freedom. In the promised land, they could experience freedom from the yoke of slavery, freedom from oppression, freedom from the burden of oppressive labor, and freedom from their surrounding enemies.

However, the first generation of Israelites did not benefit from any of these blessings as they could not rid themselves of their slave mentality. Even though they had been the subjects of heinous bondage and abuse, they were incapable of embracing the tremendous future God offered them. Their mindset was small, and they could not grasp the future generational impact God intended to perform through them. Instead, they repeatedly focused on what they saw right in front of them. Their immediate needs for food and water or potential danger from their enemies always overshadowed their ability to believe or remember the incredible victories God had previously performed on their behalf.

———

God's rest—a place of God's covenant presence
and blessing—a place of freedom.

———

Even as believers, in our humanity, if we keep blessing someone over and over but they never acknowledge or appreciate what we do, it becomes disheartening. God saw the Israelites' heart. He did not stop providing for them, protecting them, and caring for them, but He did stop their entering into the rest of a promised land.

Night Lights

My doctorate program was structured for working adults, and we had to attend four on-site residencies per school year to meet our classroom hours. We attended class typically for a week from about eight in the morning to eight at night. The campus housing arrangements were primarily for undergraduate students, so doctoral students made arrangements, mainly in hotels. Considering the intensity of the week and the need to often do schoolwork after 8:00 p.m., while staying on top of work emails or calls, I preferred staying alone.

One time just before we were to attend, the housing arrangement for a fellow classmate fell through, and he was without housing for the week. Our faculty mentor gave him her room and then told me (not asked) with amazing confidence that she was going to stay in my room for the entire week. I will spare you the details of my dismay and distress. Since it was for a good cause, and she was doing a good deed, I tried to get over myself before I arrived on campus.

Yet I was reminded of my distress on the first night. After I left the light on in the bathroom and got in the bed, she got up from her bed and turned it off. When I explained that I needed the light on so I could see in the night "to go to the bathroom," she said once again with amazing confidence the light couldn't stay on or she wouldn't be able to sleep. I meekly (but more begrudgingly) went back to bed, rolled my eyes at her in the dark, got under the covers, and put on my headphones. Because I was so annoyed, I could not see the irrationality in plotting how to turn the light back on after she fell asleep. After all, it was my room. And God knew what He was doing when He said let there be light. Where does it say that we need to turn the lights off at night? Isn't this why night-lights were invented?

The fruit of the Spirit may have kicked in as I listened to music, lying wide awake for a long time in the dark. I wondered if I would stub my toe if I had to go to the bathroom, and how I would make it to class in the morning if injured. I ended up not turning it back on, probably not because of the fruit of the Spirit but because I was too tired to get back out of the bed at some point. Either way, God knows my heart.

Despite this initial night of dismay, being jarred awake the next morning by my mentor's five o'clock alarm (of which absolutely no prewarning was provided the night before—like seriously, give a head's up), or the six o'clock "joyful noise" coming from the bathroom while she blow-dried her hair, it turned out to be a great week. I observed her sacrifice of comfort and cost as a faculty mentor to give up her room for someone else's benefit. I noted her daily discipline for 5:00 a.m. prayer every single morning, even after staying up for hours reviewing papers or preparing for a plenary lecture. I watched her calm spirit during a particularly challenging week of deadlines, pressures, and demands. I was convicted and acknowledged my own hindrances of selfishness, self-absorbedness, and reluctance to deny self.

The Hebrews author indicates reasons that prevent people from entering the rest of God. Verses 2 and 3 of chapter 4 indirectly imply that faith is needed to enter His rest, which presupposes that if faith is not present, i.e., if unbelief is present, then one did enter His rest. It says in verse 6 that some did not enter because of their disobedience. And in verse 7 it admonishes not to harden one's heart when hearing the voice of God. In summary, it highlights five key areas that will prevent us from resting in God.

*Faith is needed to enter His Rest—if unbelief is present,
one cannot enter His rest.*

Unbelief/Doubt—It is impossible to rest if we do not first believe in God. If we do not have faith in what He offers us, there is no way we can experience rest and peace in Him. If we learn more about His character, it increases our confidence when we possess an enhanced understanding and knowledge of who He is and what He stands for.

Disobedience—Disobedience occurs for a few reasons. We may disobey because we blatantly choose not to follow God, to do our own thing, and go our own way. Disobedience may occur due to our unbelief. Because we do not believe in the process and because the pressures of life we experience are so great, we lose faith or hope of things improving or turning around.

Sometimes, disobedience may occur because of impatience. We find it hard to wait on, believe, or follow God during lengthy seasons of waiting for Him to act. So we try to help things along through our own actions or following the advice and information we seek from others. Selective obedience is still disobedience.

*God wants you to rest in Him, despite how long or
how intense your problems and situations.*

Hardened Heart / Inability to Hear—A hardened heart refers to our lack of receptivity to God. If we reject the Word of God or His ways, our hearts harden. A hardened heart produces callousness to the things of God. We lose our sensitivity to hear God's voice and His promptings, to where we no longer can hear Him or recognize what He is doing.

In addition to the hindrances noted in Hebrews 4, I think two more are applicable based on the biblical example from the Israelites. The Israelites' emotions greatly contributed to how they responded to their circumstances and testing. This is similar for many believers. Based on what we see happening around us, or what we are experiencing, at times we respond emotionally in fear, anxiety, and frustration, versus standing on faith.

Fear—Fear generally relates to our discomfort to the unknown. We expect something bad or the worst to happen, or for events not to work out in our favor. Our trust in God is linked to our circumstances. The longer and more intense the trial, the greater the impact to our person, family, or overall life; it can all cause our trust to waver. We begin to think that things may not work the way we hope.

Fear also relates to our knowledge of God's character or ability to perform on our behalf. The more we know Him and His ways can contribute to increased confidence in Him. Sometimes fear is an indicator that we are not confident in Him.

1 John 4:18 says, "There is no fear in love, but perfect love casts out fear, because fear involves punishment, and the one who fears is not perfected in love." Our human emotions prevent us from

entirely trusting the purity of God's love for us based on the difficulties we face, the chaos we see in the world, and the injustices and pain so many people experience.

Anxiety—This is closely related to fear. *Oxford Dictionary* describes it as "a feeling of worry, unease, or nervousness, typically about an imminent event or something with an uncertain outcome."[10]

We do not rest based on what we have, or what He gives us, but our capacity to rest is in parallel with our relationship with Him.

When we walk with God, most of our walk is in faith. As an analytical person, I find this very unsettling—the inability to know what is coming or how certain situations will pan out. He puts us in a position to seek Him. If we knew everything, there would be little reason for us to trust and depend on Him.

The prophet Isaiah prophetically encouraged God's people when they were at an extremely dark point in their history. They were exiled from their land and the bane of all nations. But God provided them hope as well as reminded them who they belonged to in Isaiah 41:10–14:

'Do not fear, for I am with you; Do not be afraid, for I am your God. I will strengthen you, I will also help you, I will also uphold you with My righteous right hand.' "Behold,

---

10 Oxford Dictionaries and Bing, "anxiety (*n*.)," https://www.bing.com/search?q=what+does+anxiety+mean.

all those who are angered at you will be shamed and dis-
honored; Those who contend with you will be as nothing
and will perish. You will seek those who quarrel with you,
but will not find them, Those who war with you will be as
nothing and non-existent. For I am the LORD your God
who takes hold of your right hand, Who says to you, 'Do
not fear, I will help you.' Do not fear, you worm Jacob, you
people of Israel; I will help you," declares the LORD, "and
your Redeemer is the Holy One of Israel."

God provides the same hope for you today.

In the New Testament, Paul writes in Philippians 4:6, "Be anxious for nothing, but in everything by prayer and supplication with
thanksgiving let your requests be made known to God." He points
the Philippian church back to God when they experience anxiety,
worry, and stress.

> **Frustration**—This is described as "the feeling of being up-
> set or annoyed, especially because of the inability to change
> or achieve something."[11]

The longer and the more intense the problems we go through,
the more likely we will become frustrated. This emotion can ac-
company the ones above, or we can generally trust God but find
ourselves becoming irritated when things are not moving like we
want them to.

---

11 Oxford Dictionaries and Bing, "frustration (*n.*)," https://www.bing.com/
search?q=definition+of+frustration

In this regard, sometimes we will try to fix things ourselves, i.e., help God in some manner to move things along. But the wisdom shared in Proverbs 19:21 declares, "Many plans are in a man's heart, But the counsel of the Lord will stand" (also see Psalm 33:9–11).

Out of balance—A lack of balance can hinder us from resting in God. If we are out of balance or out of sync with what God is doing, it will be difficult to rest in Him. If we do not have a robust relationship, and more importantly, intimacy with Him, it is difficult to rest in Him.

———

God is a God of balance.

———

A common perspective in many churches is that the Sabbath was done away with at the advent of Christ and that it no longer needs to be practiced. However, even if the law is no longer practiced, the principle of rest still applies. Sometimes believers and ministry leaders are busy with an inordinate amount of "doing the work of ministry," but it occurs at the expense of their relationship and quality time with God—free from distraction. So, while the ministry work is needed, at the same time, it can become out of balance if minimal time in intimacy and seeking God's face is the result.

When I need to catch an early morning flight, I rarely sleep well the night before. The commute from my house to the airport, without speeding or driving like a bat in light, takes over an hour. So if my flight is at 6:30 a.m., I need to leave the house no later than 4:00 a.m. I either go to bed by 8:00 or 9:00 p.m., which of course rarely happens, or I just stay up finding things to do until I inescapably doze off at some unreasonable hour . . . usually an hour before I need to wake. The fear of oversleeping is so great that even when I do get to sleep at a reasonable time, I still wake up intermittently throughout the night, jumping up thinking I overslept. Fear and a lack of balance can be powerful drivers in one's life.

God is a God of balance. He never requires a great deal from His people without providing more in return. It is not for God that we are so consumed with work, family obligations, and household affairs; He's not the reason we end up consistently working seven days a week. Whether we work in the marketplace, in ministry, or a combination of the two, constant work seven days a week as a lifestyle is not God's plan.

Rest is ordained by God. Rest is His reward for us. Whether we choose to take a Sabbath on Saturday, Sunday, or Wednesday, we need to rest. Ceasing from our work—whether job, ministry, family, or business related—is a must. Taking a break routinely from physical and mental labor consistently allows us to reset, refresh, and start another cycle of work recharged mentally, emotionally, spiritually, and physically.

When we take a break, it is not only to step away from our work but also a time to commune with God—an appointed time designated to hear what He is saying for our present situations and fate.

Regardless of our hindrances, each of them can be considered a yoke. As discussed in the last chapter, when we take a yoke upon us, we succumb to that yoke and become subservient to it. We become subject to it as we go about our daily lives. So we can unwittingly take up yokes of unbelief, disobedience, hardened hearts, emotionalism, and imbalance, which are heavy and burdensome, instead of taking up the yoke of God. His yoke is easy, and His burden light. Will we allow these hindrances to keep us from the rest of God? Will we allow our emotions based on what we see override what we know about God and His Word? Or will we seek balance by seeking the face of God's presence so that it overshadows the interruptions that repeatedly poke us in our side and hinder us from resting fully in Him?

Reflect

* *Which hindrances impact you the most? How do these hindrances affect your ability to rest in God?*

* *What types of issues or situations influence you to be yoked to these hindrances?*

* *How can you incorporate the balance of God in your life?*

Response

Respond and journal how each of the following key principles applies to or impacts you.

* *God's rest—a place of God's covenant presence and blessing—a place of freedom.*

* *Faith is needed to enter His rest—if unbelief is present, one cannot enter His rest.*

* *God wants you to rest in Him, despite the length or intensity of the problems you are facing.*

* *I do not rest based on what I have, or what He gives me, but my capacity to rest is correlated to my relationship with Him.*

* *God is a God of balance.*

———

Rest is God's reward for me.

———

Rest

"Do not fear, for I am with you; Do not anxiously look about you, for I am your God. I will strengthen you, surely I will help you, Surely I will uphold you with My righteous right hand."

Isaiah 41:10

Father, help me to recognize and take authority over every hindrance in my life that limits, restricts, or prevents me from resting in you. Increase my faith, Lord, so that I will lean on you through all seasons and all things. Help me to trust you and look to you as the source for my rest: my provider and my refuge for peace, comfort, and strength.

CHAPTER SEVEN

A Good Night's Rest

Sweet Sleep

When I think of what a good night's rest means, I think of it as an elusive goal, something I am ever wanting, constantly needing, and rarely achieving. At times, regardless of how I aim for a minimum of six hours sleep, late work nights, business activities, ministry matters, and writing can hinder achievement of this goal. Sometimes, when I manage to get to bed at a decent hour, the inevitable insomnia will occur as it can be difficult to shut down mentally with a whirlwind of thoughts still very active and impacting my ability to fall asleep. How many of you know this to be true even when you are physically exhausted?

I wear a Garmin watch that is great for providing vitals such as steps, mileage, speed, heart rate, and calories burned for my hikes. It also provides sleep monitoring functionality when worn at night. Once you wake up, it displays your cycles of sleep—light, REM, and deep sleep. I normally can tell if I do not sleep well, but sometimes it is surprising to see when I only obtained one to two hours' deep sleep in a six- to seven-hour time frame with numerous awake times.

Some of my sleep remedies include rubbing my wrists with lavender oil, drinking Sleepy-Time herbal tea, listening to soft music, listening to books, using a lavender oil diffuser, and of course, sleeping with the light on. And when all else fails (this is shameful), when I really need to fall asleep, I read the Bible—typically Ezekiel or Revelation. God knows my heart. And believe me, it's not me—it's the devil!

My most recent remedy was purchasing a fifteen-pound weighted blanket that consists of miniscule glass beads inside. Several friends use them and highly recommended it. I must say it is working out pretty well and enhancing my deep sleep and REM time. Now I can focus on only using the Bible for its original purpose!

Aside from my weighted blanket, the remedies may aid in falling asleep but not necessarily staying asleep. Whenever I wake up from decent REM and deep sleep time, I feel like I had a good night's rest. This significantly contributes to my alertness, energy, and approach for the day. It also determines how much coffee I will end up drinking throughout the day. Unfortunately, getting a good night's rest does not happen consistently. The absence of one does not prevent me from being productive, but the presence of one certainly contributes to an easier day to navigate.

I am still on the hunt for understanding how to physically obtain a consistent good night's rest. I discovered that working up to the time I go to bed is not good, nor is drinking one liter of water within a couple of hours of retiring; it makes no sense. And using the bed as a place to do work or read at night thwarts sleep too. Aside from the annoyance of waking up from a dead sleep to go to the bathroom, the other habits keep my mind too alert to fall asleep and contribute to more restlessness while sleeping.

I continue to believe I will obtain the good night's rest of sweet sleep spoken of in Proverbs 3:24—"When you lie down, you will not be afraid; when you lie down, your sleep will be sweet."

Sabbath Rest

God provides an everlasting rest for His people. Hebrews does not simply pinpoint key hindrances to rest, but the book also provides further explanation about the Sabbath rest of God, which differs slightly from the Old Testament. Hebrews 4:8–11 (NIV) says:

> For if Joshua had given them rest, God would not have spoken later about another day. There remains, then, a Sabbath-rest for the people of God; for anyone who enters God's rest also rests from their works, just as God did from His. Let us, therefore, make every effort to enter that rest, so that no one will perish by following their example of disobedience.

These verses are interesting, as the author commingles the meaning from the Old Testament with the meaning from the New Testament.

The idea of resting from labor is now used metaphorically. He references Joshua and how He gave the Israelites' second generation rest from their surrounding enemies and led them into the promised land. However, He clarifies that the promised land was not the only rest; a rest still remained for the people of God. He says, "God would not have spoken later about another day." The other day rest that remains is still classified as a Sabbath rest, which implies the principles associated with it in the Old Testament are still applicable for this now-expanded meaning. The author also implies the Sabbath rest that remains is synonymous with God's rest. It is described metaphorically as a place, "for anyone who enters God's rest also rests from their works." While the promised land for the Israelites was equivalent to God's rest, it was also a physical place.

However, God's rest in this context refers to a symbolic place of rest, otherwise described as a Sabbath rest. God's rest is a place where we are free from works and labor, just as God rested after completing His works in Genesis chapter 1. However, in this passage, work is used symbolically and ties closely to what we discussed regarding Matthew 11. When we enter God's rest, we rest from our works. *The Amplified Bible* provides a clear description of this symbolism:

> [This mention of a rest was not a reference to their entering into Canaan.] For if Joshua had given them rest, God would not speak about another day [of opportunity] after that. So there remains a [full and complete] Sabbath rest for the people of God. For the one who has once entered His rest has also rested from [the weariness and pain of] his [human] labors, just as God rested from [those labors uniquely] His own. Let us therefore make every effort to enter that rest [of God, to know and experience it for ourselves], so that no one will fall by following the same example of disobedience [as those who died in the wilderness].

This Sabbath rest is no longer limited by physical boundaries of one day, time, or absence of physical labor. God now provides another opportunity through a relationship with Him to experience not just physical rest but an ongoing spiritual rest that is full and complete in Him.

Let us, therefore, make every effort to enter that rest,
so that no one misses it through disobedience.

We enter spiritual rest, i.e., rest in God. God's rest symbolizes a spiritual place or position. In His rest, we are in a place and a position where we are covered and protected from the enemy. God's rest is where He dwells. He inhabits a place of rest. This is an enigma, as a person who is all-powerful, all-knowing, and all-present does not actually live anywhere. However, His presence is a place of rest. In Him is rest, and His dwelling place is rest.

God's rest is where He dwells.
He inhabits a place of rest.

And just like the Old Testament promised land, this new rest and opportunity is full of blessings and promise and is overflowing with abundance. The presence of God is the rest of God and a place of promise, fulfillment, and freedom.

Repeatedly throughout Scripture we see the rest of God linked to some type of benefit, blessing, or promise. Each of the following verses reflects a sample of this linkage with a brief narrative for each.

Rest from enemies—Joshua 21:44, And the Lord gave them rest on every side, according to all that He had sworn to their fathers, and no one of all their enemies stood before them; the Lord gave all their enemies into their hand.

Rest from misfortune—1 Kings 5:4, But now the Lord my God has given me rest on every side; there is neither adversary nor misfortune.

Rest in promises fulfilled—1 Kings 8:56, Blessed be the Lord, who has given rest to His people Israel, according to all that He promised; not one word has failed of all His good promise, which He promised through Moses His servant.

Rest of God with His people—1 Chronicles 23:25, For David said, "The Lord God of Israel has given rest to His people, and He dwells in Jerusalem forever.

God's resting place—2 Chronicles 6:41, Now therefore arise, O Lord God, to Your resting place, You and the ark of Your might; let Your priests, O Lord God, be clothed with salvation and let Your godly ones rejoice in what is good.

God's resting place—Isaiah 66:1, Thus says the Lord, "Heaven is My throne and the earth is My footstool. Where then is a house you could build for Me? And where is a place that I may rest?

God's resting place—Psalm 132:8, Arise, O Lord, to Your resting place, You and the ark of Your strength.

Rest of God's favor and prosperity—2 Chronicles 14:7, For he said to Judah, "Let us build these cities and surround them with walls and towers, gates and bars. The land is still ours because we have sought the Lord our God; we

have sought Him, and He has given us rest on every side."
So they built and prospered.

Rest from pain—Isaiah 14:3, And it will be in the day
when the Lord gives you rest from your pain and turmoil
and harsh service in which you have been enslaved.

Spiritual rest—Hebrews 4:9, So there remains a Sabbath
rest for the people of God.

Believer's final rest—Revelation 14:13, And I heard a
voice from heaven, saying, "Write: 'Blessed are the dead
who die in the Lord from now on!'" "Yes," says the Spirit,
"so that they may rest from their labors, for their deeds follow with them."

Which one of the above categories speaks to you the most? How
can you apply the related scriptures to help with your ability to
rest in God?

———

*The presence of God is the rest of God and a place of promise,
fulfillment, and freedom.*

———

The list above leans heavily on passages from the Old Testament, mainly to emphasize the holistic view of rest God intended
for His people. The Sabbath rest from work and labor was just one
component. It also symbolized His heart for rest—He wants to
be your dwelling place. He gave the Israelites physical rest from

their enemies and misfortune, and He fulfilled every promise on their behalf. He blessed them with the rest of His favor, influence, and prosperity. And these meanings become fulfilled in Matthew and Hebrews when God offers those that believe in Him and accept Him spiritual rest, where we can now rest in Him and His rest be in us, which is all encompassing of everything that came before.

Nighttime

Revelation 14:13, listed in the previous section, is key as it not only points to spiritual rest in God but also has eschatological meaning as well. Eschatology refers to the study of the future of humanity and the soul, which largely goes out of this book's scope. However, it is important to at least mention it, even if briefly, as a holistic perspective of rest should at least consider its relevance. Many viewpoints on the end of humankind exist; some are conflicting, but a common premise for all is that God is sovereign, reigns over all evil, and "those who have entered into the rest of faith, by casting anchor within the veil where Christ has gone, know that the final state of rest is secure."[12]

M.C. Tenney provides a concise but robust synopsis that I find helpful without delving into the particulars of the varied eschatological theologies. He says:

> Confronted by a hostile world and by threats of repression
> if not extermination, the seer deals with the future of the
> Church in the divine plan for the ages. His first assumption

---

12 J. D. Douglas, *New Bible Dictionary*, 2nd ed., (Leicester, England: Inter-Varsity Press, 1982), 1020, entry for "Rest."

is the personality and sovereignty of God. The centrality of the throne in the Book of Revelation is a continual reminder of the superiority of God to all circumstances and persons.... His power transcends that of the persecuting state. His will determines when and how judgment will be inflicted, and His plan must triumph irrespective of the wickedness and rebellion of man.[13]

Though we seek the rest of God, and to rest in Him, this is not something we could one hundred percent realize due to our human limitations. It can only be fully actualized in the future of God's divine plan for the ages. This is the key Sabbath rest Hebrews speaks of that remains for the people of God. The kingdom of God's rest, peace, and power, though current on earth, is still not yet fully actualized.

However, this tension of the already-here-but-not-yet does not prevent us from resting in God to our fullest capacity and ability right now. The presence and spirit of God is still present and aids us when we struggle or are weak. Paul teaches us in Romans 8:26–27:

> In the same way the Spirit also helps our weakness; for we do not know how to pray as we should, but the Spirit Himself intercedes for us with groanings too deep for words; and He who searches the hearts knows what the mind of the Spirit is, because He intercedes for the saints according to the will of God.

Rest is the will of God. He mandated it. Thus, He gives us everything we need to rest in Him.

---

13 *Zondervan*, vol. 5, 98.

Place of Rest

The place of God's rest is characterized by trust. It is a place where our posture is one of complete trust in God. We are not consumed with worry, anxiety, doubt, or fear, but can simply relax in God and His promises. Psalm 37:7 says, "Rest in the Lord and wait patiently for Him; Do not fret because of him who prospers in his way, Because of the man who carries out wicked schemes." It is a place where our confidence in God is so complete that we are no longer moved by what we see around us, or the experience of others that may appear more favorably than our own. In God's rest we have the capacity to wait patiently for Him. We wait without worry, or complaining, or trying to move things along on our own as a way to help God. We can be still and wait on Him to move. We are secure in our trust in the sovereignty and rule of God over our life and the world around us.

Rest in the Lord and wait patiently for Him.

Trusting God does not mean that we just sit around doing nothing. While we wait on Him, we are still engaged and active in our relationship with Him. In the rest of God, we maintain a posture of (1) acknowledgment, (2) submission, (3) obedience, (4) discipline, (5) revelation, (6) completion, and (7) reward. It is an ongoing cycle we face as we continue to grow and mature in God. As Scripture says, we go from glory to glory in God. He tests our obedience to do just what God says even when it makes no sense, or we do not understand. Through each test we face, He reveals Himself to us as we reverence, submit to, and obey Him.

The Israelites were required to rest on the seventh day every week, as well as the seventh year, regardless of it being plowing or harvest season. Their ability to trust God despite the season—whether it be sowing or reaping season—required they obey God as well. They had to trust He would provide and meet their needs through their obedience. It did not matter if they felt tired or not, or the land was ripe for planting or not, they were required to wait and rest, not only for themselves but their animals and their land. And still today God requires that we wait as we trust Him.

As we pass and complete each test, blessings and rewards will come because of our consistent and faithful obedience. Thus, whether in Genesis, Matthew, Hebrews, or Revelation, the principle stays the same—the place of rest is a place of blessings, completion, and reward. When we dwell in a place of rest it facilitates increased ability to inherit the promises of God. It is a holy, sanctified, and separate place, as it is where God dwells—in a place of rest.

Reflect

* *When you get a good night's rest, how does this influence your day?*

* *How does each category of testing impact you: (a) test of obedience and (b) test of trust?*

* *What are you facing now that impacts your ability to rest in God? Spiritually? Physically? Mentally? Emotionally?*

* *What has God promised you if you trust and obey Him?*

Response

Respond and journal how each of these key principles applies to or impacts you.

* *Let us, therefore, make every effort to enter that rest, so that no one misses it through disobedience.*

* *God's rest is where He dwells. He inhabits a place of rest.*

* *The presence of God is the rest of God and a place of promise, fulfillment, and freedom.*

* *Rest in the Lord and wait patiently for Him.*

Rest

"Let us therefore make every effort to enter that rest [of God, to know and experience it for ourselves], so that no one will fall by following the same example of disobedience [as those who died in the wilderness]."

Hebrews 4:11 (AMP)

Father, thank you for being my hope, my provider, my source of truth, and my rest. Teach me how to obey and trust you. Help me to obey and trust in areas where I am weak or fail. Help me to rest in you and wait on you despite the bleakness of what I see. Let the rest of your presence envelop my heart and my mind so that I stand on your Word and the integrity of your character, and rest completely in you.

CHAPTER EIGHT

Morning by Morning

S O HOW DO YOU ACHIEVE A STATE OF REST IN GOD?
To be honest, you may not like the answer. I certainly do not
like the process all the time either. There is no secret sauce. The ingredients are similar in their applicability to most other Christian
principles and processes. For some these may be brand new, and
for others a reminder. Either way, there is no shortcut to pursuing
the rest of God. Like any relationship with someone we deeply
care for, it takes commitment, discipline, and focused effort.

Following are four ingredients we need to enter the rest of
God. No recipe exists related to the perfect combination, or how
much of each one we need. Nevertheless, we cannot do any one
without the others. Each one is relevant, and each one is needed in
combination with all the others.

Fervent Prayer

Prayer is a spiritual discipline most believers know about but do not robustly practice. It is something we know we should do, but we don't do it. Sometimes believers may not see the results of their prayers, which can cause discouragement and lead to a waning in their devotion. Some people may not know how to effectively pray. And in some cases, it is a lack of discipline or a lack of knowledge. Also, I do not think many ministries teach prayer as a part of their discipleship or Christian education programs, as it can become an inherent assumption that prayer in its simplest form is just talking to God, right? However, even the disciples asked Jesus to teach them how to pray.

When I announce the annual series on the topic of prayer in Bible study, it does not take binoculars to observe the dead trout stares, the diplomatic catch of some trying to keep their eyes from rolling, or the plastic smiles trying to convey this is going to be great—but mentally saying "oh great"—but not in a receptive fruit-of-the-spirit, what-would-Jesus-do kind of way. While I can teach about prayer for weeks at a time and not get bored, my enthusiasm is not always contagious. In my mind, who would not want to learn more about prayer? Why do many believers trust in prayer conceptually but do not practice it beyond a nominal way?

Without delving too deeply into the topic, I would like to focus on a few key thoughts on prayer's importance as a daily integrated spiritual practice. As with the ingredients overall in this section, prayer takes discipline, commitment, and—yes—this word again: effort. I am unable to speak about nominal relationships with God that do not experience real intimacy. But for those who desire a deeper level in God and His rest in their lives, the consistent discipline of fervent prayer is required.

Most believers understand that prayer is communication with God. The styles may vary in range across denominations and individual churches. Some denominations read their prayers, emotionally reserved and quiet, while others are more demonstratively expressive and significantly louder. Based on Scripture, there is room for both, and each has its place. And more often than not, believers will adopt the style of prayer demonstrated in the religious environments they are most exposed to or familiar with.

Consistent fervent prayer is heavily underutilized. It is a spiritual phenomenon that will benefit only those who apply effort, persistence, and tenacity. In addition to communication with God, prayer facilitates the will of God, ushers in the presence of God, and activates the power of God. When you pray, something happens. And I am not talking about the five- to fifteen-minute prayers you say when you are getting ready for work, rushing out the door in the morning, or falling asleep at night while wrapped in a duvet. I am speaking about the fervent, effectual prayer of the righteous person that avails much (James 5:16).

Prayer facilitates the will of God, ushers in the presence of God, and activates the power of God.

When we pray, spiritual activity occurs on our behalf. A disciplined prayer life nurtures time with God. If you think about your best friend, close family member, or loved one, you developed a relationship with that person after spending frequent, in-depth time with him or her. If you only spent five to fifteen minutes a day a few times a week with someone, you would probably not know them as well as if you had spent significant time together over meals, hobbies, recreational activities, or even trips.

Robust, effective prayer stokes a hunger for more of God. As we seek Him more, He reveals more of Himself to us. We learn more of His character, His process, and His ways. Thus, as we go through varying trials and issues, we increasingly trust Him more based on our increased knowledge of His character.

For example, there are people we know without any hesitation who are completely dependable. If I ask my dad for a ride to the airport, even at 6:00 a.m., I know that more often than not he will show up early and then ask me why I am not ready (um—probably because you showed up early). We know who we can depend on if we need a ride, get in a jam, or ask for help. Unless there is an emergency, they are not flaky and change their mind or renege on following through with the integrity of their word. The modern mantra of "I am doing me" supports a selfish, self-absorbed mentality that opposes the character of God.

Fervent prayer cleanses us. When we sincerely spend time with God, we abandon our motives, our agendas, and our desires and seek to hear God. Lord, what is it that you want to speak about my job, my family, my church, my business, my children, my life? What is it that you want me to do? How do you want me to respond to my issues, my concerns, my situations, or my problems? How do I address the pressures that I am facing from all sides? And what is it that you want to say in each of these areas?

Fervent prayer seeks Him, His will, and His response to us. Unfortunately, sometimes most of our prayers are spent asking. We do most, if not all, the talking, and so we miss opportunities for Him to speak to us.

Fervent prayer brings us to the heart of the Father and calms us. Once we understand and know His character—that He is dependable, faithful, incorruptible, consistent, just, and loyal—it becomes easier to relax . . . and rest . . . and be patient . . . and wait.

God spoke to the prophet Jeremiah, "'For I know the plans that I have for you,' declares the Lord, 'plans for welfare and not for calamity to give you a future and a hope'" (Jeremiah 29:11). He shared this prospect of hope when His people faced the worst odds. You may not be delivered from the problem, but He will certainly sustain you through it. Only fervent prayer orchestrates this process.

Psalm 42 is one of my favorite psalms. It has been a source of comfort for me through a number of dark times I've experienced. I share the *Amplified Bible* version below:

As the deer pants [longingly] for the water brooks, So my soul pants [longingly] for You, O God. My soul (my life, my inner self) thirsts for God, for the living God. When will I come and see the face of God? My tears have been my food day and night, While they say to me all day long, "Where is your God?" These things I [vividly] remember as I pour out my soul; How I used to go along before the great crowd of people and lead them in procession to the house of God [like a choirmaster before his singers, timing the steps to the music and the chant of the song], With the voice of joy and thanksgiving, a great crowd keeping a festival. Why are you in despair, O my soul? And why have you become restless and disturbed within me? Hope in God and wait expectantly for Him, for I shall again praise Him For the help of

His presence. O my God, my soul is in despair within me [the burden more than I can bear]; Therefore I will [fervently] remember You from the land of the Jordan And the peaks of [Mount] Hermon, from Mount Mizar. Deep calls to deep at the [thundering] sound of Your waterfalls; All Your breakers and Your waves have rolled over me. Yet the Lord will command His lovingkindness in the daytime, And in the night His song will be with me, A prayer to the God of my life. I will say to God my rock, "Why have You forgotten me? Why do I go mourning because of the oppression of the enemy?" As a crushing of my bones [with a sword], my adversaries taunt me, While they say continually to me, "Where is your God?" Why are you in despair, O my soul? Why have you become restless and disquieted within me? Hope in God and wait expectantly for Him, for I shall yet praise Him, The help of my countenance and my God.

The demands of life, the enemy's relentless taunts, and our personal challenges can drag us down a path of discouragement, doubt, and defeat. Fervent prayer consistently practiced draws us into a deeper relationship with God, which nurtures intimacy and knowing God. It facilitates faith and builds endurance. And it also provides an alternate perspective based on spiritual criteria versus our emotions and what we see in the natural. It offers us the opportunity to see our situations through the eyes of the Spirit, the power of God, and the anointing that breaks every yoke.

One final point related to fervent prayer is the need for corporate prayer. A wide-scale trend for many people who believe in God or profess Christianity is the current practice of not attending corporate worship. We learned during the 2020 global pandemic that church is not limited to a physical building, as many ministries moved their services to a virtual platform. However, virtual services, should not absolve us from regular attendance or participation in corporate services and corporate prayer, where opportunities do exist for us to attend. Sometimes the virtual services can foster sluggishness, where we rely on the replays, versus joining the live virtual service, where we actively engage in the corporate worship experience.

God is not limited to a building, but we need to still engage corporately. Hebrews 10:24, 25 (AMP) admonishes believers:

> And let us consider [thoughtfully] how we may encourage one another to love and to do good deeds, not forsaking our meeting together [as believers for worship and instruction], as is the habit of some, but encouraging one another; and all the more [faithfully] as you see the day [of Christ's return] approaching.

Lone ranger fervent prayer or individual bedside worship in our homes could never compare to the power and spiritual authority of corporate connectivity.

In *Innovative Prayer Leader*, C. Terrell Wheat outlines four key reasons corporate prayer service should be a part of our prayer life:

1. It breaks the spirit of fear off a church. (Acts 4:29)

2. It becomes the place of power. (Matthew 18:19)

3. It releases a distinct sound. (Acts 4:31)

4. It reverses the plans of the enemy. (Acts 12:5)

Further he teaches, "Nothing frightens the devil more than the people of God coming together to call on their Father for help. Corporate prayer says to God 'we need help.' It says to the devil, 'look, joker we have help.'"[14]

It is a deceptive plan of the enemy to weaken the body of Christ through lukewarmness, passivity, separatism, and division. The less we gather corporately, the weaker the links for connectivity and power in the body of Christ, and the more leverage the enemy has to attack. If you do not attend anywhere corporately, consider asking God to guide you to a place of worship made just for you and your family. The body of Christ needs all hands on deck—and that includes you—like never before.

For a greater understanding and deeper dive into tactical aspects of prayer, prayer approaches, and the value of corporate prayer, I recommend the following resources, which I refer to when teaching:

- Becoming a Prayer Warrior by Elizabeth Alves

- Intercessory Prayer by Dutch Sheets

- Just Pray by John F. Hannah

Hopefully your receptivity to these prayer resources and openness to learn more about prayer is met with an authentic, gregarious smile that radiates "I am doing what Jesus would do"—in text language, LOLBVS (laughing out loud but very serious).

---

14 C. Terrell Wheat, *The Innovative Prayer Leader* (Kindle, 2020), 67.

Declaration

The Word of God is a key ingredient. It is God's will to perform His Word in your life. But in concert with Him performing His Word is the need for us to declare it. Jeremiah 1:11 says, "Then the Lord said to me, 'You have seen well, for I am watching over My word to perform it.'" If God watches over His Word to perform it, it implies that the Word must be present in some form for Him to watch it. It needs to be spoken. The Word carries power and when spoken, intrinsic power occurs as it's released. Even when we read the Word (aside from any use as a sleep aid), it normally refreshes, revives, and brings life as it is read to the reader. So, in turn as it is spoken, power is released spiritually and supernaturally. We are unable to naturally explain the process or how it is done, but our main responsibility is to speak and declare the Word in and over our circumstances.

I use the word *declaring* rather than *speaking*. Speaking works; however, to declare the Word means to speak it with authority and faith. Declaring the Word emphasizes that we recognize it is God's Word spoken to a situation, and it will enforce victory for His divine purpose. When we pray and declare His Word while praying, spiritual activity takes place for our targeted request through supernatural means, as highlighted in Scripture in the Old and New Testaments. Psalm 103:20 says, "Bless the Lord, you His angels, Mighty in strength, who perform His Word, Obeying the voice of His word." And Hebrews 1:14 shares, "Are they not all rendering spirits, sent out to render service for the sake of those who will render salvation?" God's Word is performed as angels of the Lord obey the voice of the word that is spoken.

We pray more effectively when we include the Word. The Word aligns with God's will; thus, as we declare the word it is already in sync with God's divine purpose.

A conundrum of emotions, experiences, external voices, and cultural nuances can shape what we think and how we think. All these influences can contribute to the effectiveness of how we respond to life and its challenges. There are so many voices, and depending how much time we spend listening to them, they can directly impact our ability to listen to one singular voice—God's. Whether we are listening to the voices we hear via television, social media, news, entertainment channels, or people who mean well but are not biblically sound or spiritually discerning, we can miss what God wants to say or do in our life and circumstances. If we do not take time to know God or His will, our emotions, trials, temptations, and other distractions will strongly influence our ability to rest in God.

God's Word, the Bible, is truth. His Word is impartial and provides parameters for our conduct, listening to God, and discerning His voice amid great darkness and deception that is widespread on the earth. What feels good, what is rational (or rationalized), and what makes sense have become norms for truth. However, truth may be uncomfortable, unpopular, and may not always make sense based on what is culturally trending. John 8:31–32 says, "If you continue in My word, then you are truly My disciples; and you will know the truth, and the truth will set you free." We can only rest in God as His disciples when His Word is a part of our rest. His Word provides a standard on which we consistently rely. Everything else that influences us is subject to change and untrustworthy.

Interestingly, when we studied how one does not enter God's rest due to disobedience in Hebrews 4:11, immediately following in verses 12–13, it says:

For the word of God is living and active, and sharper than any two-edged sword, even penetrating as far as the division of soul and spirit, of both joints and marrow, and able to judge the thoughts and intentions of the heart. And there is no creature hidden from His sight, but all things are open and laid bare to the eyes of Him to whom we must answer.

Thus, it is imperative to be acquainted with His Word. It is the point of reference to gauge the appropriateness of our feelings and behavior, as well as what we hear and permit to feed and nurture us mentally, spiritually, and even physically. It is difficult to maintain a position of rest when the majority of what we listen to, or watch, encourages our carnal emotions, unhealthy thoughts, and ungodly responses, rather than the development of our spirit and character. For many it is easier to visit social media numerous times a day or binge-watch television shows and movies for hours at a time than it is to sit still for thirty minutes in God's presence daily, or sit in a corporate worship service for sixty to ninety minutes, one day per week.

Hebrews 6:17–18 further admonishes us:

In the same way God, desiring even more to demonstrate to the heirs of the promise the fact that His purpose is unchangeable, confirmed it with an oath, so that by two unchangeable things in which it is impossible for God to lie, we who have taken refuge would have strong encouragement to hold firmly to the hope set before us. This hope we have as an anchor of the soul, a hope both sure and reliable and one which enters within the veil.

Our ability to hope and to hold firmly to our faith must be tied to the guideline of His Word. It is the direct authority whereby we invoke it in our fervent prayer, praise, and worship. All are interdependent.

Stillness & Meditation

Stillness and meditation go hand in hand with prayer and the Word. As our prayer lives transition from less asking to more listening, we are first quiet, and then still. Being still is a posture of listening, waiting and expecting to hear from God. If we are always on the go, inundated with work and other activities, it is difficult to develop the sensitivity and consistency of hearing from Him.

It reminds me of the Elijah narrative in 1 Kings 19. Elijah had just experienced one of the greatest encounters and breakthroughs of his prophetic career, but when the queen threatened to kill him, he ran in fear. While he hid in a cave, God told Elijah that He would pass by in a visit. A strong forceful wind came, but God was not in the wind. A huge earthquake came, but He was not in the earthquake. Then a fire came, but He was not in the fire either. Instead, God came in a gentle blowing. He passed by in the stillness of a soft whisper.

God wants to speak to you. He wants to speak to you about your work, your burdens, your pains, and your fears. Not just physical labor but the spiritual impact as well. As believers, we labor in the spirit as we encounter the wind of spiritual warfare, face the earthquakes of spiritual battles, and engage in fiery spiritual conflict. At times, these experiences are excruciatingly intense. But in taking a break, fervently praying, and being still in His presence, we reset.

The posture of stillness does not mean do nothing. Psalm 46:10 says, "Cease striving and know that I am God." Other translations such as the *New International Version* and *Amplified Bible* use the phrase "Be still." And the remainder of the verse then says, "I will be exalted among the nations, I will be exalted in the earth." Our stillness is a posture of not only listening but also of reflecting upon the majesty of our God. As we reflect on His character and remember the good things He has done, it will draw us into peace and rest in His presence.

———

When we intentionally take time to rest from the physical, we proactively use this time to commit time for stillness in His presence.

———

Stillness is the process of stopping our busyness and remembering God. Taking time to think about Him, appreciate Him, and celebrate His goodness. It is meditation. Sometimes I get nervous saying we need to meditate, as this word has been hijacked by many other belief systems that do not include God in their equation. In this spiritual context, I refer to a biblical foundation for meditation where God is always included as a part of our remembrance and reflection as described in each of the following verses:

Joshua 1:8—This book of the law shall not depart from your mouth, but you shall meditate on it day and night, so that you may be careful to do according to all that is written in it; for then you will make your way prosperous, and then you will have success.

Psalm 1:2—But his delight is in the law of the Lord, And in His law he meditates day and night.

Psalm 27:4—One thing I have asked from the Lord, that I shall seek: That I may dwell in the house of the Lord all the days of my life, To behold the beauty of the Lord And to meditate in His temple.

Psalm 145:5—On the glorious splendor of Your majesty And on Your wonderful works, I will meditate.

1 Timothy 4:15—Take pains with these things; be absorbed in them, so that your progress will be evident to all.

And while we focus and rely on biblical truth as our foundation and source for meditation, it is not surprising that secular research supports the practice and promotes the benefits as well. According to Mayo Clinic:[15]

> Meditation can give you a sense of calm, peace, and balance that can benefit both your emotional well-being and your overall health. And these benefits don't end when your meditation session ends. Meditation can help carry you more calmly through your day and may help you manage symptoms of certain medical conditions.... The emotional benefits of meditation can include:

- Gaining a new perspective on stressful situations

- Building skills to manage your stress

- Increasing self-awareness

- Focusing on the present

- Reducing negative emotions

---

15 Mayo Clinic Staff, "Meditation: A Simple, Fast Way to Reduce Stress," April 22, 2020, https://www.mayoclinic.org/tests-procedures/meditation/in-depth/meditation/art-20045858.

- Increasing imagination and creativity

- Increasing patience and tolerance

Some research suggests that meditation may help people manage symptoms of conditions such as:

- Anxiety

- Asthma

- Cancer

- Chronic pain

- Depression

- Heart disease

- High blood pressure

- Irritable bowel syndrome

- Sleep problems

- Tension headaches

Not that we need research to prove or even validate biblical principles, but is it not uncanny, or rather miraculous, the significant value God orchestrated in the principles He designed for those that believe and follow them?

These appointed times of stillness and meditation include listening and documenting what God says to us for reflection and activation as He directs. The discipline of stillness eases us into His presence as students who sit at His feet to listen and learn from Him as He speaks. When we intentionally take time to rest from the physical, we proactively use this time to commit time for stillness in His presence. To still our busyness and still our thoughts and reflect on Him. To be still and seek His face.

Praise & Worship

Meditation and stillness can take practice to develop. For many people, sitting still is difficult. To sit without the distraction of checking your cell phone, perusing social media, turning on the television, or following up on some random task that always comes to mind as you start can be uncomfortable. One way to overcome this is the act of praise and worship. These do not need to be limited to just corporate worship. They are effective ingredients to usher in the presence of God whether in your home, car, or wherever your location.

I see praise and worship as two separate activities, although mutually inclusive. Praise is the act of thanking God for what He has done, is doing, or will do. It is a celebration of the acts of God—what He does. Whereas worship is the act of adoration of who God is—a celebration of His character and nature. Both are demonstrative, whether through singing, lifting the hands, waving the hands, dancing, or other like displays.

In our personal time with God, we may or may not be as demonstrative as in a corporate service, but our personal praise and worship still holds value. It can be as simple as listening to praise and worship music and using it as a means to facilitate stillness in the presence of God. If listening is not in competition with the aforementioned distractions, the same process for reflection, remembrance, and meditation on God are still applicable.

Praise

In his message "The Power of Praise in Times of Trouble," Dr. Charles Stanley outlines a number of tenets on praise he believes are key for believers:[16]

- The safest place in the midst of difficulty is to be in the presence of God and thinking about Him.

- When we turn to Him, we are recognizing the Sovereignty of God.

- We recall the mighty acts of God when we praise Him.

- We acknowledge our weakness and our dependence on Him.

- Praise enlarges our vision of God to beyond the natural.

- Praise oftentimes is the prerequisite for knowing the will of God.

- Praise fills the heart with the *joy* of the Lord.

16 Charles Stanley, "The Power of Praise in Times of Trouble," InTouch Ministries, https://www.intouch.org/listen/featured/the-power-of-praise-in-times-of-trouble.

Many times we are unable to rest in God because we focus so much on our circumstances, issues, and consuming thoughts of what could go wrong. Thus, we are unable to see God in our circumstances, how He actually may be at work, or be thankful for the "little" things He has done. Praise facilitates the process of us focusing our mind upward and on God, versus downward on us and our situations.

Worship

Worship transcends our focus to adoration and reverence of God without thought to His acts. We worship Him as He is holy and separate. We honor Him as sovereign. Many of the Psalms illustrate worship of God, such as Psalm 29, Psalm 84, and Psalm 96. Psalm 96:7–10 says,

> Ascribe to the Lord, O families of the peoples, Ascribe to the Lord glory and strength. Ascribe to the Lord the glory of His name; Bring an offering and come into His courts. Worship the Lord in holy attire; Tremble before Him, all the earth. Say among the nations, "The Lord reigns; Indeed, the world is firmly established, it will not be moved; He will judge the peoples with equity."

The focus is on His glory and presence.

Worship centers us on God. It draws us into His presence. It draws us into reflection. And it draws us into stillness and rest. In some corporate settings when the glory of God is so present, it brings a "holy hush." As the prophet Habakkuk declared, "But the Lord is in His holy temple. Let all the earth be silent before Him" (Habakkuk 2:20). There is nothing we can say, nothing that needs to be said lest God speaks. Some people feel compelled to bow or kneel. Some lie prostrate in His presence. Regardless of form, a deference to His presence occurs. His presence brings rest.

Worship centers us on God. It draws us into His presence. It draws us into reflection. And it draws us into stillness and rest.

In conclusion, to enter the rest of God, we must actively pursue four ingredients—fervent prayer, declaration of God's Word, stillness and meditation, and praise and worship—on an ongoing basis. Due to our humanity, we will experience times when we struggle in our emotions, wane in our commitment, or are too weak to stand. However, we must persevere and continue in our faith. Psalm 116:7 says, "Return to your rest, O my soul, For the Lord has dealt bountifully with you." The rest of God is a place we continually press to remain as we face pressure from all around that may routinely unseat us from our posture of rest in Him. But each time you get off balance, knocked down, or knocked out, repair—restore—relief—refresh—reset—and rest.

Reflect

* *Which of the four ingredient(s) studied in this chapter (fervent prayer, declaration, stillness & meditation, praise, & worship) do you struggle with the most? Why do you struggle with these the most?*

* *Which ingredient(s) do you use most effectively and why?*

* *How will you take steps to incorporate these ingredients into the daily discipline of your life?*

Response

Respond and journal how each of the following key principles applies to or impacts you.

* *We need to intentionally seek rest on a regular basis.*

* *Prayer facilitates the will of God, ushers in the presence of God, and activates the power of God.*

* *When we intentionally take time to rest from the physical, we proactively use this time to commit to being still in His presence.*

* *Worship centers us on God. It draws us into His presence. It draws us into reflection. And it draws us into stillness and rest.*

Rest

"And the Lord gave them rest on every side, according to all that He had sworn to their fathers, and no one of all their enemies stood before them; the Lord gave all their enemies into their hand."

Joshua 21:44

"Return to your rest, O my soul, For the Lord has dealt bountifully with you."

Psalm 116:7

Lord, thank you for this increased knowledge and wisdom. I want to know you in an intimate way. I want to learn of you and seek your face. Increase my desire and discipline for prayer. Create in me a burning passion for praise, worship, and your Word. And help me to still myself in your presence—to meditate and listen for your voice. Lord, I want to know you. Help me to know your voice from my voice, the enemy's voice, and all the other voices that distract and deter me from entering the fullness of your continual daily presence of rest.

CHAPTER NINE

In His Rest

I CONTINUE TO SLEEP WITH A DIM LIGHT ON. NOW IT IS not so much fear as it is convenience. Whether I'm going to the bathroom or reaching for a book or pen, the dimness versus complete darkness makes it easier to see. This is my story, and I am sticking to it.

But victoriously, my sleep continuously improves as my ability to rest in God increases. Instead of lying awake in stress or worry, I rest in the confidence of God's presence and power to move. Instead of working seven days a week at my job and ministry work, I take breaks that include time with God, self, family, or friends. Instead of being inundated with worries, emotional burdens, or spiritual concerns, I learn and seek to arrest my thoughts and lay them on the altar. I proactively pursue rest and purposely trust God as I seek to align my lifestyle with His principles of rest.

Snuggles

My granddaughter comes to mind as a quintessential example of perfect sleep. Even in a king-size bed, she makes sure she sleeps on every single inch of the mattress before she wakes up the next morning. This occurs regardless of whether others are in the same space. She does not see us as obstacles or even as an inconvenience as she carries on soundly sleeping, with us becoming a part of her mattress.

Other times, she lays her full portly body horizontally across the pillow. Unfortunately, my head is always still on the pillow. She settles in to sleep for the night on the pillow with her entire body across the top of my head. Aside from the fact that I can barely breathe, I also can hardly talk with her entire belly pressed into my face as I forcibly muffle, "I can't breathe" or "Can you please move over?" Her only response is to partly raise up, look at me blankly while sucking on her pacifier, and then go back to laying across my entire pillow on top of my head. And then probably to antagonize me even more, she proceeds to pat my back repetitively as if she is putting me to sleep versus the other way around. Even when I move her over to keep from dying an untimely death from belly smothering, she still inevitably finds her way during the night back to the pillow, horizontally stretched out across my head.

In her one-year-old wisdom, that was her best way of staying close to me. Resting next to me was not enough. Having her pick of two other pillows that did not have my head on them was not enough. Even sharing my pillow and lying right beside me was not enough. She snuggled up as close as she could get, where she thought I would be unable to move, get away, or be disconnected from her during the night—on top of my head.

The Call

God extends a call to you through this study. Whether you have walked with Him for decades, a few years, or just started your journey with Him, He is either reminding or calling you to come closer. Despite the chaos in the world around us, we must keep moving toward Him. Regardless of what it looks like around you, what you are facing, or how you feel, in Him is rest. There is no other way.

There are no shortcuts or quick routes. Hindrances can no longer become obstacles or inconveniences that deter us from fervent prayer, the Word of God, praise and worship, and stillness and meditation. Instead, obstacles need to become a nonentity in the landscape of our spiritual mattress as we rest in Him. Plow through each with focus, tenacity, perseverance, and steadfastness. Our desire for Him and to please Him should increase and draw us to a place where we commit to press in toward Him beyond our emotions, what we see around us, or what we face.

In God is rest. Are you willing to accept His call to rest in Him? Are you willing to pursue submission, obedience, and discipline?

In her book *Discerning the Voice of God*, Priscilla Shirer sets out her thoughts related to the key reason some believers' walks are so different from others:[17]

Have you ever met someone whose relationship with God is so full, robust, and real that his or her life seems more like a spreading wildfire than a quietly contained religion? *I have.* . . . They fascinate me, these individuals who are

---

17 Priscilla Shirer, *Discerning the Voice of God: How to Recognize When God Speaks* (Nashville: LifeWay Press, 2017), 28.

radically unique even among other Christians I know. There's just something deeper and more substantial about their walks than the rest of ours. They have a firm unshakable resolve in God, and their experiences with Him ... I always take time to ask them what they'd pinpoint as the main reason behind their ongoing fervor. And without fail, their answers are remarkably similar. (It always makes me wonder: if the secret is really so evident, why aren't we all doing the same thing?) Here's the repeated theme: *their walks with God aren't centered primarily on knowledge; they hinge on a relationship experience* . . . dedicated to aligning their lifestyle with it.

Many times, our knowledge of God limits our walk with Him due to discomfort, inconvenience, or strength. If we know little, we may experience little.

But as believers, we need to embrace the mindset that in His rest comes a daily determination and effort to die to self. Matthew 16:24 (AMP) says:

Then Jesus said to His disciples, "If anyone wishes to follow Me [as My disciple], he must deny himself [set aside selfish interests], and take up his cross [expressing a willingness to endure whatever may come] and follow Me [believing in Me, conforming to My example in living and, if need be, suffering or perhaps dying because of faith in Me].

We can never experience the full rest of God without denying ourselves.

Self-denial allows room for God to reveal Himself to us as we take up His cross and complete His work in us. This comes through commitment and our honoring a covenant of relationship with Him. He desires more than just belief or knowledge of Him. He desires a lifestyle of intimacy with Him—a lifestyle—versus nominal interactions based on convenience.

In God's rest it may be inconvenient to practice the daily discipline and effort of fervent prayer, declaration, stillness, and praise and worship. It may be a bother to attend corporate worship weekly with loads of work, personal demands, and other obligations on our weekends. It may be painful to our pride to walk in the fruit of the spirit with those who may not deserve our kindness, grace, or mercy. But the rest of God is experienced in a lifestyle of committed obedience, trust, and intimacy where we snuggle up to Him as close as we can.

Do you accept God's call for a lifestyle of rest in Him?

Rest

"Come to Me, all who are weary and heavy-laden, and I will give you rest. Take My yoke upon you and learn from Me, for I am gentle and humble in heart, and you will find rest for your souls. For My yoke is easy and My burden is light."

Matthew 11:28–30

Father, thank you for your revelation and wisdom. Thank you for drawing me to you and revealing more of yourself to me. Thank you for loving me enough to call me to come closer to you not just in knowledge, but drawing me into your heart, into your face, and into your presence. Help me to experience you on another level of trust, obedience, discipline, and intimacy like I have never experienced. I accept your call to a lifestyle of rest in you. Amen.

Afterword

THE IDEA FOR THIS BOOK WAS BIRTHED FROM A fast. The original reason for the fast was completely unrelated to writing a book, which was nowhere in my mind. I did it during a time of great transition, loss, distress, and anxiety. Desperate times call for desperate means, and I felt led to fast to cleanse and free myself from distractions. I needed to clearly hear and understand what God wanted to say during that season. Though He did not remove my distressing circumstances, He gave me great grace and strength to plow through them.

On the last day of the fast, I heard in my spirit "the rest of God." My first notion was that it was just a thought, which would have been extremely disappointing after days of denying myself food; but as I continued to wait, I understood "the rest of God" to be a book topic. God wanted me to write a book about resting in Him.

Weeks went by, then months and years, but I made no progress on the book idea. Routinely, I would receive some type of idea or thought pattern for the book. I would write down those ideas along with other random content as I received it.

In time I recognized I was walking out and learning the lessons firsthand myself. Aside from my sleep exploits, over the years I experienced deeper levels in God through suffering, disappointments, and trial and error. Each of these provide credibility and support for the principles identified in Scripture and explained throughout this book.

In my last year of working as a director in a top-tier consulting firm, I learned the rest of God in the face of a dark, inequitable, unscrupulous work environment where I could not fend for myself. I had to bend the knee and suppress my right to fight directly. I sought for the righteousness of God through indirect channels of justice and fairness to prevail over the backroom conversations and water cooler chats where my name was being dragged down. I learned that in the face of insurmountable odds, loss of reputation, risk of livelihood, and missed opportunities from disingenuous communications, the favor and influence of God is like none other. He can turn a situation around and produce a miracle on your behalf like you can never imagine.

The moment we give up fighting, let go of trying to figure it out, and release our control is the moment of greatest opportunity for God to use His glory to shine. It is the time for the rest of God to come into our hearts and come upon us.

Pandemic Musings

I wrote this book during the 2020 pandemic. The impact of the pandemic was not limited to only the United States, but it impacted nations across the globe. Although some nations were able to address and navigate the unchartered waters of the pandemic better than others, it did not stop the wide-scale impact of COVID-19. In addition to the hundreds of thousands of people who lost their lives to the coronavirus, millions more suffered from the impact of the virus in other ways, whether physically, socially, or economically. Millions of people lost their jobs, thousands of businesses closed, and economies around the world were shaken. All these issues negatively impacted not only individuals but also families, communities, and entire nations across the globe.

In addition to the virus, the summer of 2020 in the United States was particularly characterized by significant civil unrest, violence, and crime. Despite the peaceful protests that occurred across the nation, many were disrupted by violent counterprotests, as well as strong displays of extreme hatred. Regrettably, on top of the effects of the virus, many more people, and particularly businesses, continued to be impacted by the civil unrest as well.

Throughout this season, between the propagation of social media, news sources, and political interests, rampant controversies occurred over truth, exaggeration, and untruth, which incited vast levels of fear. Consequently, significant levels of anxiety and frustration were prevalent. Unprecedented quantities of suicide, domestic disputes, domestic abuse, and child abuse occurred.

Given the extreme difficulties many Christians faced, coupled with their fear, stress, and anxiety, many struggled with their faith, with some shaken in their belief system and view of God. These trials were compounded by the inability to attend in-person church programs. Remote attendance through social media or platforms like Zoom became the new normal for the main touch points of corporate worship. This period significantly tested and tried believers, but it was also a staunch example of the enormity of affliction many believers endure on an ongoing basis in other parts of the globe.

Personally, during this year, I navigated six months of unemployment while I completed my doctorate degree. Of course, at the beginning of these months, there was zero hint of a forthcoming pandemic that would lead to millions of people losing their jobs and a nationwide recession. As my cash reserve dwindled, I aggressively applied for jobs despite the unemployment rate rising exponentially on a weekly basis. Thoughts filled with fear and doubt routinely tried to grip me, but I consistently arrested them before they planted and took root in my mind. Thoughts will come, but it is up to us how to respond.

During this season, I experienced many difficulties, but as I maneuvered through each of those situations, I found grace. Instead of anxiety or fear, peace and rest undergirded me through this season of loss and uncertainty. Aside from the loss of a dear friend to death, my inconveniences were miniscule compared to the suffering so many around the world endured. Thankfully, offers eventually came and I was blessed in the midst of a pandemic despite millions of people being unemployed. It set the stage for lessons learned in resting in God.

If you enjoyed this book, please consider posting a review on Amazon. Even if it's only a few sentences, it would be a huge help: https://www.amazon.com/dp/1736311123/

CPSIA information can be obtained
at www.ICGtesting.com
Printed in the USA
LVHW031201240621
691050LV00004B/241